Is this you?

"If only they would just sit still. . . "

"It's too hard to constantly manage the kids during Mass. . . "

"Why should I worry about my kids? They're mostly quiet. Besides, I go to church to feel good about myself. . . "

You don't need a special "knack" to have quiet, orderly children who kneel in the pew during Sunday morning Mass. You don't need an advanced college degree to be a good parent. You can change their behavior by applying consistent, firm, and loving expectations of them.

This workbook will show you the way. We'll talk about the importance of good behavior as well as *how* to change your children's behavior.

If you and your spouse are willing to invest some time and effort ...

If you are willing to change . . .

If you recognize that things could be better, but you're not sure where to start . . .

Be prepared for a refreshing change. You—and everyone around you—will ultimately get more out of Mass.

This workbook is the place to start.

About the Author

Michael J. Rayes is a native of Arizona, a lifelong Catholic, and a husband and father. Rayes earned his bachelor's degree in education, and holds two master's degrees, one in business administration and the other in professional counseling.

Rayes is the author of two action-mystery stories for Catholic kids, Bank Robbery! and Papal Bull Heist. He is the past president of three civic and charitable organizations. Rayes is a licensed professional counselor and the clinical director of Intercessory Counseling & Wellness.

28 Days

to Better Behavior

28 Days

to Better Behavior

HOW TO HAVE ATTENTIVE KIDS AT MASS —
AND PEACE IN THE PEW!

Guaranteed results!
If their behavior doesn't change in 28 days,
you'll get a full refund!

Michael J. Rayes

RAFKA PRESS
Phoenix, Arizona

Balloon quotations used throughout this book are taken from *The Book of Catholic Quotations,* John Chapin, ed. (Fort Collins, CO: Roman Catholic Books), original pub. 1956, copyright renewed 1984 by Farrar, Straus & Giroux, Inc.

Scripture quotations are taken from the Douay-Rheims version, 1899 edition of the John Murphy Company, with Challoner revisions of 1749–1752. Available online at www.drbo.org.

Copyright © 2011 Michael J. Rayes
Graphics and illustrations copyright © 2011 Laura Rayes

All rights reserved. No part of this book may be reproduced or transmitted in any form or by any means, electronic or mechanical, including photocopying, recording, or by any information storage or retrieval system now existing or to be invented, without written permission from the author, except for the inclusion of brief quotations in a review.

Published by

Rafka Press LLC
Phoenix, Arizona, USA

ISBN-13: 978-0-9779628-4-6

10 9 8 7 6 5 4 3 2 (August 26, 2023)

Library of Congress Control Number: 2010911040

Rafka
Press

Visit us online at www.rafkapress.com
For more information: info@rafkapress.com

To my wife, Laura,
the one person who persevered with me, grew with me,
and learned how to raise kids with me.
I love you.

"Suffer the little children to come unto me, and forbid them not; for of such is the kingdom of God."

— words of Jesus Christ (Mark 10:14)

Contents

Icons used throughout this workbook

There are several graphic icons in the margins of this book. Each icon represents a different "tip" or nugget of useful information. These bits of advice come from Catholic teaching and sound psychology in raising well-behaved children.

Grandmother - Parenting tip. This icon points out parenting skills you may learn from a sweet little old grandma who is full of wisdom—and apple pie.

Halo - Good behavior. See this icon for advice on how to make children behave.

Pitchfork - Bad behavior. This icon highlights causes of bad behavior in children.

Stars and circles - Unfocused kids. This icon marks advice for dealing with kids who have trouble focusing on an activity.

Clouds - thoughts of Heaven and God. This icon denotes points to ponder about Higher things.

Disclaimer and guarantee

This book is designed to provide information on child discipline and parenting, particularly applied to the celebration of the Roman Catholic liturgy on Sunday mornings. The book carries a guarantee that, in a normal two-parent family, child behavior will improve in 28 days if the information presented herein is followed. However, it is sold to you with the understanding that neither the publisher nor the author is engaged in rendering counseling, legal advice, or other professional services. The author of this book is not a licensed counselor and is not a psychologist. If such expert assistance is required, the reader is urged to seek the services of a competent professional.

Every effort has been made to ensure the completeness and accuracy of this book. However, there may be mistakes, both typographical and in content. This text should be used as a general guide for the subject matter covered, not as the single source of parenting information.

The purpose of this book is to inform and entertain. This book outlines methods and strategies the author has learned as a Catholic parent to facilitate improvement in child behavior over the course of 28 days. The author and/or Rafka Press LLC are neither liable nor responsible to any person or entity with respect to any loss or harm caused, or alleged to have been caused, directly or indirectly, by the information contained in this book.

If you do not wish to be bound by the above, you may return this book to the publisher for a full refund.

Author's notes about this book

When writing this book, I could have utilized the APA citation style when documenting quotations and referenced works. Some readers will say I should have used APA, since this little book is basically a parenting manual, which means it has a lot of psychological and pedagogical concepts in it. But I wanted it to be *readable*. The book is intended for a popular, general audience; not a group of researchers or doctors. Thus, I used the Chicago style throughout the book.

Another point worth mentioning: I used the words "teach" and "train" somewhat interchangeably, although they mean different things. To *teach* is to impart knowledge. To *train* is to form by instruction, drills, and guided practice. Teaching involves learning relatively deep concepts, while training involves learning a skill.

Sometimes I used the words interchangeably, as I mentioned above, but generally I used the word "teach" to imply handing on knowledge about the liturgy or love of God, and "train" to imply instruction in good behavior skills.

One last point: Some of the people cited in this little book are Catholic (like Doctor von Hildebrand), some became Catholics before they died (like Doctor Adler), and some are not Catholic at all and probably never will be (like Doctor Dobson). It's all about context. I've taken the good things written by these authorities in their fields, and incorporated them into the context of making children behave well for Sunday Mass. This certainly doesn't mean I agree with everything they say on other topics.

– M.J.R.

Foreword

The Kingdom Needs Children

Suffer the little children to come to Me.

Suffer. Sometimes that's the word that comes to mind when I traipse into church leading a chain of small children. My diaper bag is bursting with books, blankies, and binkies. I'm hoping that for once I am not too late to get a good seat—in the back.

Sorry! The back pew is already taken. *Again.*

It seems like every parish I've visited has a contingent of old folks who arrive early and fill up the back rows. My family can't even dream of beating them to church. The old folks get there when it's dark, and open the doors with their own key. Meanwhile I'm still at home combing bed head out of kids' hair.

I've always wondered what prompts them to sit in the back. Perhaps they've heard the gospel of the publican and the pharisee one too many times. (The thumping noises which I thought were coming from the heating system are really them beating their breasts.) Or maybe they're the type who sat in that pew for so many years that they've gotten attached to it—literally. The stained glass windows in the church say "Gift of." The back pews say "Property of."

Yet do they really need it? Except for the occasional gab session, these people generally behave themselves. Unlike my attention-challenged children, seniors do not play with the hair of the people in front of them. They are not given to wandering the aisles, hopping over the pews or dumping the contents of purses all over the floor.

I used to dream of a parish that would reserve the back pews for families. What other recourse do people with small children have?

The confessional? Tried to nurse a baby in there once. Too cramped and stuffy.

The choir loft? Too dangerous for the little dare-devils and uh, the choir isn't looking for *those* kind of voices.

The basement? The stairwell? The roof? Might as well stay home and watch EWTN.

What about the crying room?

Ah! I must admit it's a peaceful solution for the rest of the parish (which no doubt, generously endowed it). I personally think it's a great incentive for parents to control their children. If you leave your pew because your child is threatening a mini-riot—what's it like in the crying room where the inmates are in charge of the asylum? In the parish of my youth the holding cell was right up front just off the sanctuary. There parents felt the added incentive of being on display behind glass, rather like monkeys at the zoo.

Long ago I realized that there was just nowhere to hide. That's why our family sits up front.

You read that right. We sit right up front.

I'll be honest with you. We started sitting up front because it was the only place left. But God always knows what He's doing, even when it seems to make no sense to us. Sitting up front forced us to train our children to behave. More importantly, instead of trying to pray *in spite* of our children, we now pray *with* our children.

If you are a parent like me and wish you could bring your children into the Eucharistic Presence of Jesus not only physically but *spiritually*, read on. The bite-size approach in this book is easy to use on your bite-size people. (And if you're a really frazzled parent, your bite-size brain.)

Don't have small children yourself? Thinking of getting the book for that harried mother hiding bed head under her veil—the one whose kid kicked your pew a total of 73 times last Sunday?

Remember that Our Lord was talking to the apostles when He used the word "suffer." He knew that kids drive adults crazy. Without Him our natural impulse is to banish the kids.

I was recently at a parish which is blessed with many families. It has a policy wherein families with noisy kids get "benched" outside the church—sometimes in seats where they can't even see. I was once standing in the back of that church rocking my child on my hip. Even though my child was quiet and we were in nobody's way, an elderly parishioner with a distinctive hairy eyeball, directed me outside to the bench where there was much wailing and gnashing of Cheerios.

I felt excommunicated.

One Sunday the priest dedicated the majority of his sermon to telling parents the various ways the children were driving everybody crazy. They were noisy and fidgety, they drowned out the sermon, they ran the bathroom relay. Not only that but they spread cupcake crumbs far and wide at parish suppers. Not only *that* but urchins like these followed this priest around and sat next to him at fine restaurants where they fiendishly commenced hollering, climbing, and playing bumper cars with the chairs.

I thought to myself, now here's a true apostle! Definition— someone who thinks preaching the gospel would be a heck of a lot easier if the kids would just go home where they belong.

Enter Jesus. Suffer the children is the gospel for our times. Of such is the Kingdom of Heaven. Perhaps it's because they challenge our notion of piety. They turn around and gape into our faces and get into our comfort zones. They shake us out of our complacency.

Children need the Kingdom and the Kingdom needs children.

That's even more true today. In the late fifties my parents had to stand in line to enroll my oldest brother in Catholic school. Shortly before I, the youngest of the family, left eighth grade in 1980, the school closed for lack of e

nrollment.

In our current parish, which is Ukrainian, there are few children. Elderly parishioners worry about keeping their beloved parish open. Many have expressed their anxieties to us. Once, not long after we joined, we had to go out of town. The following Sunday more than one parishioner said, "I'm so glad to see you. We thought maybe you'd left the parish." What did we have that attracted them to us? Children. Lots of them.

Contrast this to the parish mentioned above which has many families making sacrifices every day to bring up children according to the Faith. Where in the rest of the world will you find such people willing to suffer, to bring hope for the future of the Church and the world? Unfortunately, these days parishes like that are rare.

Perhaps it was this that prompted the apostle above to add a final word to the child-free adults in his congregation - the same ones who had apparently been stuffing his complaint box of late. "Offer it up."

For our part, parents should teach proper behavior. With the help of this book, many will make progress, I'm sure. Yet, there will still be times when kids will act like kids and not mini-adults. At those times, I hope people will remember the words of Our Lord, "Suffer the children."

Many a Babushka has winked at our successive, rambunctious two-year-olds over the years. I've no doubt that wink is a prayer.

— Susie Lloyd
Author of *Please Don't Drink the Holy Water!*
and *Bless Me Father, For I Have Kids*

Introduction

A personal story

Someone urgently poked my shoulder. I turned around and saw fire in her eyes. She was an old, plump lady, the sort who moves slowly but is excited easily.

She bared her fangs and began hissing.

"Discipline your child!" she whispered hoarsely. Flecks of spittle flew out of her mouth as she wheezed at me. She was breathing hard. There I stood in the pew during the reading of the gospel — the priest and altar servers in front of me, hundreds of fellow Catholics surrounding me, and a belligerent old woman behind me. I was about to whisper to her to back off and mind her own business when I looked down at where she was pointing.

My three-year-old son lay on the pew, his chubby legs up in the air … and my open pocket knife in his hands. He had reached into my pocket and pulled it out without my noticing.

I gasped and quickly retrieved the knife. I made him sit up, although that only lasted about ten seconds. I could hear the fire-breathing old lady muttering something behind me while the priest continued reading the gospel.

That was ten years ago. Today, the chubby little boy is a teenager, and my seven children never have the opportunity to reach into my pockets during Mass—because they all face forward while standing, sitting, and kneeling when the adults do.

Children *can* behave at Holy Mass, and it doesn't hurt them. Respectful, quiet behavior is tremendously good for their developing characters and has benefits in other aspects of their lives. It took me many, many months—actually, a few years— to get my children to behave properly during Mass. And the Mass I'm talking about is not a loud Mass for youth, either. My children attend the traditional Latin Mass every Sunday, and during parts of it, the building full of 300 adults and children is so quiet you can hear a rosary clink against a pew from the other side of the church.

You don't have to wonder how to make your children behave at Mass. You don't have to anguish over which strategy is the best to take, as I did. You don't have to spend years achieving better behavior from your children. I can show you how to have well-behaved, respectful children at even the quietest, most reverent Sunday liturgy. And it will only take four Sunday Masses. That's 28 days.

So now . . . let's get started.

God loves us more
than we love Him.

Chapter 1

What is the Holy Sacrifice of the Mass?

Before we tackle the subject of children's behavior at Mass, we should first look at the basics.

While Christ our Lord walked this earth 2,000 years ago, He not only gave instruction to men, He gave them very clear examples. One lesson He taught is what mortal sin really does to God. It hurts Him. It offends Him. The Second Person of the Blessed Trinity came to earth so He could become the perfect Victim to atone for our sins. The gates of Heaven were closed to men; not even a just man could enter Heaven. The just who died were waiting in a limbo of natural happiness (also known as "Abraham's bosom"), but they could not enter Heaven.[1] Someone had to atone for Adam's broken relationship with God. But it was really broken, and all men fall short of the perfection of God. No one could restore this relationship.

No one, that is, except God Himself. See how much He wants us? See how badly He wants us to love Him? That's why He made us in the first place.

Therefore, the Second Person of the Triune God—Jesus Christ—came to earth to offer Himself to God the Father, as a perfect sacrifice to open the gates of Heaven. He became man so a man could atone for the broken relationship, and open Heaven! He could have done this simply by the humiliation of becoming a man. He could have done it at His circumcision, since His blood was shed. He could have done it when He started his public ministry as an adult. But He wanted to show us the evil of mortal sin.[2] He was whipped, scourged; mocked and crowned with long thorns; handed over to merciless executioners; and finally hung on a cross like the worst of criminals (indeed, two of the worst highwaymen were finally caught and hung on two crosses next to Him).

We were held by the wisdom of the serpent, but we are freed by the foolishness of God.

— St. Augustine: *De Doctrina Christiana*, I, 14, 13.
4th Century

> God could have
> become an angel, but He
> became a man instead.

Christ died once for sinners, according to sacred scripture (1 St. Peter 3:18). However, men live in each generation. Christ died, rose again, and ascended into Heaven almost 2,000 years ago. His perfect sacrifice stretches forth as an eternal Now, regardless of time or generations of men. Thus, everyone from Adam to the last man on earth can apply the fruits of Redemption. But how do we, those in the merely, early 21st Century? How did Catholics do it in 1810? How did they do it in the year 510? How do we enter into this eternal Now and see Christ on the cross, and ask Him to make His sacrifice for us?

> To me, nothing is so consoling, so piercing, so thrilling, so overcoming, as the Mass. It is not a mere form of words—it is a great action, the greatest action that can be on earth. It is, not the invocation merely, but, if I dare use the word, the evocation of the Eternal.
> —Cardinal Newman: *Loss and Gain*, 20.
> 19th Century

The answer is the Holy Sacrifice of Mass.

The Mass is the re-presentation of the one sacrifice of the cross. It is Redemption applied today.[3] It is an unbloody sacrifice, but it is the same sacrifice.[4] God teaches us in the Mass of the Catechumens, as Jesus Christ instructed men during His public ministry; and God redeems us in the Mass of the Faithful, as Jesus Christ offered Himself to God the Father while hanging on the cross.

Therefore, Holy Mass is the way we human beings on earth come to Calvary. This is how we kneel at the foot of the cross, with Blessed Mary and Saint John. It doesn't matter that we didn't live 2,000 years ago—we can kneel at the foot of the cross every time we attend Mass. We offer ourselves in the pews when the priest acts *in persona Christe* and offers Jesus Christ, as the sacred Host, to God the Father.[5] It is Redemption. It is Christ our Savior opening Heaven for us. It is Now. We are on God's time when we are at Mass.

God Himself is eager to help you teach your kids respect during Mass.

This is basic Catholic theology. But a practical consideration comes into question. What is proper behavior during Mass? Should we simply "come as you are" (like the evangelical Protestants) or does this incredible event demand something of us? Should we be noisy, or silent?

Attending Mass is not like attending a ball game or going shopping. One's participation in the majesty of God's sacrifice to Himself requires nothing less than awe in His presence. That is why we are quiet in the church and we dress up for Mass. The Council of Trent actually decreed that bishops should banish "vain and therefore profane conversations, all walking about, noise and clamour, that so the house of God may seem to be, and may be called truly a house of prayer."[6]

The late Dietrich von Hildebrand, an expert on the liturgy who was called a "twentieth century Doctor of the Church" by Pope Pius XII, wrote, "Reverence is the mother of all virtues, of all religion."[7] While reverence in the liturgy includes a spirit of awe before the majesty of God, Doctor von Hildebrand further pointed out that true reverence during Holy Mass "is full of the spirit of *servire Domino in laetitia,* of serving God in joy."[8]

That is why it's important for our children to behave and show quiet respect for God in the tabernacle, and not be a distraction to others.

An investment—and the payoff

From a business perspective, let's look at this as an investment. If I invest X, what will it get me? If I invest money, how much Return on Investment (ROI) will I get in 12 months? If I invest time, how much money will I save? If I haven't bought my wife flowers lately, I need to invest in my marriage. (The ROI in marriage is huge!) And if I invest heavily in good child behavior, what is the ROI? Let's take a look.

Investment
Four weeks of consistent
child discipline and behavioral training

Results
Good kids at Mass
without constant discipline

Duration
Several weeks until
major event, like a new baby

Let's say you spend four weeks following the instructions in this book, and your kids change their behavior at Mass. ROI should begin at week five, but will only last until some major event happens in your life. By that time, you will need to reinforce behavioral training again. Don't worry—it won't take you four more weeks! Reinforcement only takes a Sunday or two. Let's say that two and a half months after your kids have adjusted to your proactive, disciplinary approach to good behavior, you have a new baby or the kids' grandmother dies or you move to a new house. That's ten weeks of good behavior that needed maintenance by you, to be sure, but did not require such a heavy amount of instruction and discipline as the first four weeks.

Investment

Four weeks of training

Results
Good kids at Sunday Mass

Duration
Ten weeks (using example above)

Return on Investment of four weeks:

Ten weeks of good behavior

[Fourteen weeks total time,
minus four weeks of investment]

Not bad, eh? If nothing major happens to change your children's sense of security, you could be in "maintenance mode"—a little discipline or correction here and there—for many months until you really need to go over things with them again. And remember, reinforcing your behavioral principles won't take 28 days again. It will require one or two Sundays of vigilant discipline on your part, and probably one day during the week when you talk about behaving during Sunday Mass.

Let's put it another way. If you want to grow a garden, do you simply throw some seeds down, water them, and walk away? Probably not, if you want a nice garden! You plan the garden out in your mind first, or even draw a diagram of it on paper, and then rake and break up the dirt. You want all the weeds and grass out of the way. You may even fertilize and enrich the soil before you plant and water. Do you need to prepare the soil every week? Of course not. You did it once and now you water the seedlings and pull weeds now and then.

Next Sunday, look down your pew. If you have a young family, you are growing a garden of souls for God. Mother Teresa of Calcutta once asked, "How can there be too many children? That is like saying there are too many flowers." So, let's enrich the soil

Your kids will behave better when they aren't at Mass, too.

and prepare the garden! You'll be a happier parent for having done it. As Saint Francis de Sales once said, "It is a great honour to you who are married that God, in His design to multiply souls who may bless and praise Him for all eternity, causes you to co-operate with Him in so noble a work."[9]

Benefits of good behavior at Mass

Probably the most obvious benefit of learning how to behave at Mass is a child's ability to behave in other places

handsome kids who put on their best behavior? Sign me up!

as well. Children do not compartmentalize their lives as adults do. If Mommy or Daddy says something on Sunday, it means the same thing on Tuesday. You may notice it is easier to control your kids when dining at a restaurant or while grocery shopping. Yes, they still need direction, but they will listen to you now.

Another benefit is that your children will learn to focus. This is a huge issue today. Children are exposed to visual media such as TV and video games. They are also over-stimulated with constant movement, especially if they are shuttled around in a vehicle every day. It's hard for them to focus on a single activity. Teaching them to behave well at Mass (especially facing forward even when they are bored) trains them to focus on one thing.

Your children will understand that certain situations in our civilized society require them to act and dress differently. They cannot always chew gum with their mouths open and wear casual clothes.

Sounds good, doesn't it? Do you want well-behaved children? Do you want them to grow in the love and knowledge of Jesus Christ, our Lord? You already bring them to Sunday Mass. Do you want them to behave better while they are there? Let's take a closer look at your children and where you should seat them inside the church.

[1] St. Thomas Aquinas, *Summa Theologica*, Supl. Q. 69, art. 4. From the New Advent online edition: http://www.newadvent.org/summa/5069.htm, Also cf. *Catechism of the Catholic Church*, no. 633.

[2] *The Catechism of the Council of Trent* (Rockford, IL: TAN Books and Publishers, Inc., 1982) pp. 50–51 & 57; cf. *Catechism of the Catholic Church*, 457–460.

[3] Council of Trent, Session XXII, I. From *Dogmatic Canons and Decrees* (Rockford, IL: TAN Books and Publishers, Inc., 1977) pp.132–133.

[4] *The Heart of the Mass* (Kansas City, MO: Sarto House, 1997) p. 5.

[5] Ibid., p. 47.

[6] "*...vana atque adeo, psana colloquia, deambulatioes, strepitus, clamores arceant, ut domes Dei, vere domus oratiois esse videatur et dici posit.*" From the original conciliar documents (Cologne: apud maternum cholinum, published 1564). Council of Trent, Session XXII, IX. Cf. *Dogmatic Canons and Decrees*, p. 147.

[7] Dietrich von Hildebrand, *Liturgy and Personality* (Manchester, NH: Sophia Institute Press, 1990) p. 49.

[8] Ibid., p. 55–56.

[9] Francis Johnston, *The Voice of the Saints* (Rockford, IL: TAN Books and Publishers, Inc., 1986) p. 101.

Chapter 2

Temperament and positioning

I wrote this book with a "nuclear family" in mind: A mother, a father, and several children. If you are a single mother, you can still elicit better behavior from your children at Mass, but it will take more than 28 days. An adult friend or relative will be a big help in the pew.

Parents with misbehaved children often do not position them correctly in the pew. On the other hand, parents with well-behaved children almost always position themselves well. Here are two examples:

Dad   Mom   boy   boy   boy   boy   girl

The kids are naughty, unfocused, turn around in their pews, and generally distract everyone.

boy   Dad   boy   boy   Mom   girl   boy

The kids are much better behaved. They usually don't turn around, and they kneel when they should.

If you change your seating arrangement in the pew, that strategy alone will make your children behave better. How is the father supposed to keep an eye on his sons if they are out of reach?

Create the best seating

Your children know exactly how far your arms can reach, and they act accordingly.

arrangement for your family by knowing your children and placing them strategically by their temperaments and their ages. Temperament? Is that like personality? Yes and no. **Temperament** is what someone is *inclined* to do because of how they are wired. **Personality** combines temperament with the learned habits of a person. So, temperament is how you were born, but personality is what you became. Since children—especially small children—do not yet have fully developed personalities, let's take a closer look at temperament. This is important if you want to know your children well, and understand what makes them "tick."

If we consider the reaction of various persons to the same experience, we will find that it is different in every one of them; it may be quick and lasting, or slow but lasting; or it may be quick but of short duration, or slow and of short duration. This manner of reaction, or the different degrees of excitability, is what we call 'temperament.' There are four temperaments: the **choleric**, the **melancholic**, the **sanguine**, and the **phlegmatic**.[10]

It is somewhat rare that a person is purely one temperament. Most people have a mixed temperament, but one temperament tends to dominate the other.[11] Thus, you may have a sanguine-choleric child and a choleric-melancholic child. You may want to study the four temperaments to understand

yourself and your children better, but here is a quick snapshot
of some dominant character traits in each temperament:[12]

Sanguine The laugher	Optimistic, flirty, shallow, sociable, prefers group activities, extraverted, active, excites easily but quickly forgets
Choleric The doer	Ambitious, argumentative, insensitive, self-confident, strong initiative but low endurance, usually extraverted, very active, excites easily and remains strong and lasting
Melancholic The worrier	Introspective, avoids groups, prefers to work and play alone, lacks self-confidence, moody, frets and worries, introverted, passive, excites slowly but deeply
Phlegmatic The thinker	Slow, lazy, distant, mood is constant, indifferent to external affairs, peaceful, sluggish but has strong endurance, introverted, passive, excites slowly but shallow and tends to forget

You probably already have an idea that your children
have different temperaments, especially if you have a large
family. One child is reserved, another is hyperactive and
explosive, and another never stops talking and laughing. Two
children who tend to be light-hearted and outgoing should not
sit next to each other during Mass. A serious case of the giggles
will erupt at the most inopportune moment.

The root of the matter does not lie in texts: it lies deeper:
it lies in the character of every man.
— R.H. Benson: *An Average Man*
20th Century

Some psychologists advocate a theory that birth order
makes a permanent impact on personality. Doctor Kevin

Leman makes a very compelling case that birth order "gives us many clues about why people are the way they are."[13]

Birth order means that the first-born child will respond differently to situations than the last-born. The middle child in the family will respond differently than other children. The second-born child typically feels to be "in a race" with the first-born, who received more individual attention from the parents.[14]

Many first-borns are choleric, and many last-borns are sanguine.

Here are a couple seating arrangements I recommend when attending Mass with your family. They take both birth order and the classical four temperaments into consideration:

Melancholic-Phlegmatic older child / Sanguine younger child / Father / toddler / Melancholic-Phlegmatic older child / Sanguine older child / Mother / baby

In the above arrangement, the mother can sit at the end of the pew so she can make a hasty exit if the baby starts to make noise.

The next seating arrangement is for a family with a father who tends to discipline more than the mother.

Sanguine-choleric teen / Melancholic–Phlegmatic younger child / toddler / Father / toddler / Choleric older child or teen / Melancholic–Phlegmatic older child or teen / Mother / older child (any temperament)

Notice that in both examples, the toddlers never sit next to Mom. This works well in a family with a calm mother and a somewhat high-strung father. Why? Because the calm mother can be soft. While this works well during the week because of her natural tenderness, she might be too tolerant during Sunday Mass. They need to be on either side of Dad, who should have the endurance to keep focusing them on the Mass. Sometimes, a toddler may demand to sit next to Mom. The toddler will insist on it and you may sense a tantrum coming on. Use this to your advantage, Catholic Dad. Lean over and whisper to her.

"If you read from your prayer book for the next five minutes and kneel really still, then you can sit next to Mommy. OK?"

See how that works. Most of the time it will; sometimes the tantrum will happen anyway, and then Daddy must take her out.

One spouse in most marriages tends to be more laid-back about child discipline, and the other spouse tends to be the active disciplinarian. In the above examples, the father disciplines, the mother is laid-back. What about your marriage? Who tends to have a lower tolerance of misbehavior from the kids? Sit the younger ones next to that parent. The older children can sit next to the calmer parent.

To reduce fighting, pair up calm and hyper kids.

Use the lines on the next page to decide which one of you tends to be the "disciplinarian" and which one tends to be more lax. Write your names in the appropriate field. If both of you tend to have similar roles, or if you tend to be stricter with certain children, you can write that down as well.

Name of Parent	Role
_____	_____
_____	_____
	(Disciplinarian, lax, patient,
	impatient, etc.)

Notes

_____

_____

_____

_____

Next, use the chart below to write the names of all your children, oldest to youngest. Decide what you believe is their dominant temperament. Here is an example.

Name of Child	Temperament
Joseph	*Choleric–Phlegmatic*
Johnny	*Choleric–Melancholic*
Jake	*Sanguine*
Jenny	*Melancholic*
Jessica	*Choleric–Sanguine*

Your family:

Name of Child	Temperament
_____	_____
_____	_____
_____	_____
_____	_____
_____	_____
_____	_____
_____	_____
_____	_____
_____	_____

Temperament Cheat Sheet

Sanguine: Clowns around, outgoing, friendly, dramatic, mood swings, active

Choleric: bossy, insensitive, ambitious, active

Melancholic: Introspective, introverted, worries a lot, moody, lacks self-confidence

Phlegmatic: slow, lazy, calm, passive

In my opinion, it is better when the father enforces discipline. If that isn't the case in your marriage, perhaps the two of you can discuss child discipline together, and see if there is a better way. In some families, the father is the doting, fun parent, while the mother is the one who sets limits. To the Catholic wife and mother, if this describes you, and you are comfortable in that role, fine. But if you harbor a secret desire to have your husband pitch in, set boundaries, and be the enforcer, sit down after a nice, relaxing meal together, and talk with your husband!

Notice also, in the recommended seating arrangements, that the gender of the children has nothing to do with where they are seated. It doesn't matter if your child is a boy or a girl. What really matters is their temperament. Who clashes with whom? Children who tend to have a lot of friction shouldn't sit together. Oftentimes, it is because their temperaments clash. If you have a large family, you can also use their age ranges to your advantage. Place older children next to younger children. Have the older children help the younger ones focus on the Mass.

In both seating scenarios earlier in this chapter, the mother and father are strategically placed (especially the father) so they can reach the "high maintenance" children easily.

Now, decide who will sit next to whom. Visualize a pew in your church. Where will everyone sit? Use the chart below to plan it out. Write the names of your family members in the spaces where you want them to sit for Sunday Mass.

End of Pew

End of Pew

____ ____ ____ ____ ____ ____ ____ ____

What if you have a small family, or there is only one parent at Mass? Try this arrangement:

Sanguine child / Melancholic child / Mother / Choleric child

The sanguine child has the end seat, so he can see the altar better. Sanguines tend to have focusing issues, so this seat may help. Having the choleric child next to the parent will help curtail the child's natural bossiness from irritating the other children. Or, depending upon the age of the child, you may *want* to put an older choleric child next to a much younger child—the older choleric could help the younger child follow a prayer book.

Entering the church

Review one or two rules with your kids before you even go inside the building. Stand at the door of the church and remind them that they need to go inside quietly, and they must all genuflect (like you practiced at home this week).

Open the door and go inside the church. You may want to arrange your children single-file in the order in which you will seat them. When the door to the vestibule closes, it shuts out the world. Inside God's house, there is nothing but quiet reverence for our

If you tell your kids ahead of time you expect them to be good, their behavior usually improves.

Savior. Each child should genuflect and then get into the pew. Everyone should immediately kneel down and silently say their prayers.

Do not let them sit. (You will have to remind them of this outside the church door.) This focuses their attention right away.

Redemption applies to everyone in the church building, from the tiniest baby to the oldest great-grandparent.

They should not fumble with anything. No rosaries, prayer books, Missals, nothing. Just kneel for at least 20 seconds to help them focus on the silence of God's house, and then they can take out their rosaries and books.

It's far more natural and simple to like beauty. Every child does.
— R.H. Benson: *The Dawn of All*
   20th Century

Now that you've got your kids seated appropriately in the pew, they have to remain there for at least an hour! Don't worry, it can be done. God gave you these children, and He will give you the grace you need to raise them well. Yes, you can do this! You are already a parent, so you are the most natural teacher for them, at least until they reach adolescence. You are also the most natural person to discipline them. God established human nature that way. You don't need a special "knack" or advanced education. You can raise your kids well and train them to behave reverently at Sunday Mass. Read on to learn specific strategies for keeping them in the pew—quiet and orderly.

---

[10] Rev. Conrad Hock, *The Four Temperaments* (Milwaukee, WI: The Pallottine Fathers & Brothers, Inc., 1962, reprinted 2002) page 7. Emphasis in original.

[11] Ibid, page 48.

[12] Ibid, pages 7 and 53–55. Also, *The Four Humours* (from the World Wide Web: http://www.kheper.net/topics/typology/four_humours.html. Note: This is definitely NOT a Catholic site, and it shows.)

[13] Kevin Leman, *The Birth Order Book* (New York: Dell Publishing, 1985), p. 15.

[14] Child Development & Parenting Information, "Birth Order," online at http://www.childdevelopmentinfo.com/development/birth_order.htm.

Chapter 3

Active participation

In 1947, Pope Pius XII warned all the bishops of the world that some people were agitating for radical changes in the liturgy.

> [C]ertain enthusiasts, over-eager in their search for novelty, are straying beyond the path of sound doctrine and prudence. [They mix] their plans and hopes for a revival of the sacred liturgy with principles which compromise this holiest of causes in theory or practice, and sometimes even taint it with errors touching Catholic faith and ascetical doctrine.[15]

A decade and a half later, the Second Vatican Council emphasized "full, conscious, and active participation" of the laity as the main reason for changing the liturgy.[16] After the council, enthusiastic liturgical planners interpreted "active participation" to mean "a lot of noise and activity for the laity." Hand-clapping and handshakes were introduced for the first time in the 2,000-year history of the liturgy. However, active participation does not require a buzz of activity at the redeeming sacrifice of the cross renewed on the altar at today's Holy Mass. What is really needed is the participation of the heart, as Pius XII wrote in his encyclical letter on the sacred liturgy.[17]

How does this participation of the heart manifest itself? For a small child, it means kneeling when the adults do. It means

While at Mass, look at a statue of Jesus or a holy card and think about His Sacred Heart.

watching the priest and the altar boys. It means reading only certain books at Mass — lives of the saints, children's Catholic books by Father Lawrence Lovasik (the more traditional ones), or a child's Missal. You are training the child's heart to become used to the Mass; to think of Sunday Mass as a solemn event. You are teaching your children to respect the Mass, so they will grow to love the divine Author of the Mass.

Your children have a right to attend Mass, if they are baptized Catholics. Don't be afraid to bring them inside the church to attend Mass with you. They have a right to be there, no matter their ages. When the baby begins to cry, you'll have to take him outside or walk him around the back, or utilize the cry room if your parish or chapel has one. I generally recommend that parents start out with the baby inside the church, and only take him out if needed.

What does all of this do for your children as they become young adults?

Bring your children to Mass every week for at least 18 years, and you'll make a permanent impression on their soul that will never go away.

If your adult children stop attending Mass when they move out of your house, it will feel strange to them. They will lie awake at night, because they don't "feel" right. They will be orphans out on a limb. Thanks to your consistent Mass attendance, and your strategic discipline to make them behave and pay attention, they will never feel quite right in their hearts when they skip Mass. This is a wonderful thing—you're laying the foundation for a return to God's one true Church if they were to stray as they mature and grow older! How ironic—your children would be miserable but it would be a good thing—like the prodigal son before he came to his senses.

Your adult children will, by the grace of God, remain faithful and grow in sanctity from a childhood of prayer and good training. Let's look again at good training and active participation for your children.

You may have to **tolerate** bad behavior from your adult children, but you should never **accept** it.

Kneeling

During Mass, yes. Absolutely. How old do they have to be to kneel? Generally, two-years old, depending upon the precocity of the child. Every child in the world, except those with developmental concerns, can kneel at a Latin Sung Mass throughout the entire canon by the age of three, and a Low Mass by age four. If you attend the new Mass in English, the "canon" is the Eucharistic Prayer. During the Eucharistic Prayer, your children should stay in the pew with you, and kneel when everyone else does.

Should children kneel before Mass for devotions? It depends upon the length of the Mass. If you know it will take a long time and there will be a lot of kneeling, you may want to let them sit. This is for children about seven and younger. They only have so much endurance.

By the time a child has reached the "age of reason" (typically, seven-years old), he or she should kneel as much as the adults for devotions before Mass. What if your eleven or twelve-year-old boy wimps out and doesn't kneel correctly? What if you, as a Catholic mother, are

When your kids play during the week, watch their knees. They can certainly kneel for an hour.

exasperated with his laziness and you are tired of nagging him? If he has lazy-butt syndrome, have his father talk to him after Mass. Older girls with similar posture should also be talked with after Mass.

Whatever you do, don't let your children kneel on the kneeler with their bottoms resting on the edge of the pew behind them, even if it's during devotions before Mass. This posture encourages laziness among the young. If they see older adults thus kneeling, gently explain that their elders cannot kneel upright for very long because their knees or back hurt them, which is probably quite true. If it isn't true, then . . . um . . . well, get off the pew!

Pew Sitting 101   3 Graces
Prerequisites: none
SU 9:00-10:00 AM
Location: St. Acrimonious Church

Course Description: How do you sit in the pew when grumpy old people are kneeling behind you? It's very simple—sit at the edge of the pew, and do NOT lean back! If you're a toddler, Mommy or Daddy can even let you sit up on the kneeler.

As you try different strategies for each of your kids, you'll discover what works best. I use doughnuts as weapons. A few years back I had a four-year-old who was stubborn as a mule. Removing him from church, spankings, scoldings, discussing behavior before Mass, making him sit still after Mass—none of it worked. I was perplexed. Finally I carried through with a threat to withhold doughnuts after Mass. He had to sit there while everyone else in the family had doughnuts. He asked for a doughnut several times, and I reminded him each time that he could not have one because of his bad, disobedient behavior during Mass. Next week he'll get one if he's good.

I was astonished at his excellent behavior from that point forward.

Watch the priest

Focus, focus, focus. Your little five-year-old isn't there to stare at the pew in front of him and fidget. Remind him every once in a while to look up at the priest and the altar boys. What is the priest doing? Oh, watch the altar boy carry that

"He studied motivation in one of his college psychology
classes. Now he uses doughnuts as weapons."

big book! You're holding a book, too. Did you read it? Look at the pictures. Look up, now the priest is turning around and extending his hands.

Let us fear the Lord Jesus, Whose blood was given for us; let us respect
 our leaders; let us honor the presbyters; let us teach the
young in the school of the fear of God.
— Pope St. Clement I: *Letter to the Corinthians,* 21,6.
    1ˢᵗ Century

Books to read

This is critical if you want well-behaved children! Bringing children to Mass empty handed is like going out in the rain without an umbrella. Or getting ready for a job interview when you suddenly realize your best suit is dirty. In other words, *you haven't prepared well.* Get a bunch of books on the saints by Father Lovasik. Most of his books align very well with the practice of the traditional Latin Mass, but some of them show examples from the new Mass in English (such as *My Picture Missal* and *Receiving Holy Communion*). Get a good children's Missal or prayer book. You can even bring a picture bible.

Kids sit still when they read or watch TV. Guess which one is better for them.

Do not bring Winnie the Pooh books or other secular books; you want them to understand that this is God's house, it's the Lord's Day, and we are on God's time. Wait a few minutes after you enter the church to pass out books. Be a control freak. Keep all the books. Then, give each child *one* book. When they are done reading it, don't worry—they'll let you know. Trade books with them. By the time Mass is over, all the younger children will have read all the Lovasik books, their hand Missals, pages they tore from your expensive gilt-edged Missal, the parish bulletin, and the warning label sewn into your baby bag. Twice.

Eating during Mass

Should your toddler eat dry cereal or raisins during Mass? Your little ones can perhaps go a few hours without eating, but it depends upon a growth spurt they may experience, if they are feeling well, and how much they ate the night before. A safe bet is to feed them *before* Mass, so you don't have to feed them during Mass. If you are using food to distract them during Mass, stop. Give them quiet toys, books, and laminated holy cards instead.

A few years ago, I cut round corners on a bunch of our plastic holy cards so our baby and toddler could play with them during Mass. No more sharp corners. I then used a hole-punch to put a single hole in each one, and ran them through a big plastic ring. Now there's a ring of holy cards for them. They don't get lost as easily.

> If you use food to distract your child, keep him busy, or make him feel better, he will weigh 300 pounds by the time he turns 19.

If you are pressed for time—of course you are pressed for time! It's Sunday morning and you're getting ready for Holy Mass!—feed them granola bars, cheese sticks, or Pop Tarts in the van on the way to church. (Or something without much sugar.) School-aged children who already made their first Holy Communion should fast before receiving. Talk to a good, traditional priest if you have any questions.

Toys and rosaries—to a kid, they're the same thing

Ah, the joy of kidhood. Everything is a toy, nothing is dangerous, and money comes from the bank, not hard work. What do you do when you're bored at Mass and Mommy gives you a rosary? You bang the beads against the wooden pew, of course! It gradually gets louder and louder and LOUDER until you get the Mommy Glare. Then you stop.

What was wonderful about childhood is that anything in it was a wonder.
It was not merely a world full of miracles; it was a miraculous world.
— G.K. Chesterton: *Autobiography*
20th Century

I would only entrust a rosary to a toddler at Mass if she held it quietly. I sure wouldn't let a child have a Hot Wheels car at Mass. Yes, rosaries are good things. So is cheesecake, I guess. But I wouldn't let a three-year-old bake me a cheesecake, and I'm careful about who gets a rosary at Mass. Maybe you can give your daughter a rosary when she's a little older and quieter. (She should definitely use the rosary every day at home, with the rest of the family.) Older children should definitely have rosaries and hand Missals during Mass.

The front pew—the best seats in the house!

After a while, once your kids achieved a minimum level of orderly behavior, seat them in the very front pew. It sounds scary, but they do behave better up there. They can clearly see the action at the altar, which captures their attention. You can also get some mileage out of it, if you milk it:

"Now Jenny and Johnny, you're up here in the very first pew! Everyone—everyone can see you! The whole congregation will know if you are behaving or not. So be extra good today. Look, you can see the candles on the altar!"

Woo hoo! You're raising the standard.

Go east, young man

Traditionally, a Catholic church building faces east—an architectural plan known as *ad orientem*—so the sanctuary and altar are against the eastern wall, and the vestibule is at the western side of the building.

Kids aren't as bored at an event if they can **see** the front of the church, auditorium, or the theater. If their view is blocked, they'll get fidgety.

In many Catholic churches and chapels, an unfortunate thing happens. Families toward the front of the church tend to have relatively better-behaved children, but families toward the rear of the church tend to have poorly behaved children. Why? A vicious cycle is taking place: Families who sit up front tend to take the liturgy a bit more seriously, while families in the back may not be as devout. The children, who are very perceptive, act accordingly. Since the children don't behave well, the parents never want to sit up closer, and since they never sit up closer, the children never improve their behavior.

First, the parents' attitude must change. Then they can begin choosing a better pew, which will help the children pay attention. The front two pews are best.

Another thing that may help them focus: When Mass ends, wait a minute or two so you (and your kids) can say your thanksgiving prayers, and most of the doughnut-starved congregation can clear out. Then walk the children up to the communion rail. This is especially good for preschoolers who haven't made their first Holy Communion. Have them kneel silently at the railing for a minute. As an adult, it's easy to forget that when you're only three feet tall, you can't see the altar around all the big people in the pews ahead of you. The communion-rail visit will also help them focus at Mass. If you don't have a communion rail at your church, bring them to the front pew instead.

More than once, I was exasperated with my children's fidgetiness and generally **Kids need to pray too.** uncooperative behavior at Mass. So I made them all kneel down quietly for about five minutes in the living room when we arrived home Sunday afternoon. This teaches them two lessons:

- Kneeling at Mass is important.
- Since they didn't kneel correctly at Mass, it's taking away from their play time at home.

I explained to them that we owe kneeling time to God, since He is our creator and so good to us. We must visit His house and attend Mass on Sundays, and we have to kneel during parts of the Mass. If you don't kneel at Mass, then you have to kneel here at home.

What if they talk while they're kneeling at home? I charge them a minute a word.

"But Daddy…"

"Oh, that's two more minutes. Shhh! Don't add any more minutes. Just kneel there quietly."

That strategy works well. Most of the time, you can make them kneel after Mass on the kneeler in church, if needed. I decided to use the "kneel at home" strategy to really reinforce the importance of kneeling.

Holy Mass—it isn't just for Sundays anymore

You may want to take your kids to Mass during the week, too. This has spiritual benefits for everyone in the family. If you can't attend daily Mass, what if you went one day during the week? Maybe every other Wednesday? Or Saturday? If you want to get better at something, you have to practice. It took months for me to learn enough tennis to hit the ball over the net 90 percent of the time. Similarly, it takes practice to learn a musical instrument. Good behavior at Mass is no different—so why not take advantage of the opportunity on a day other than Sunday? Weekday Masses usually draw less people and are only 30 to 40 minutes in length.

Practice makes perfect. Bring your kids to Mass more often.

Besides attending Mass on a weekday, you can do other things during the week to improve your children's behavior on Sunday morning. You can help them focus! You can role-play with them! I'll discuss these strategies in the next chapter.

Mass planner worksheet

A plan for more Masses and less messes

Use this worksheet to prepare for attending Holy Days of Obligation and a weekday Mass.

Upcoming Holy Day of Obligation:

_____

Which day can we attend a weekday Mass this month:

_____

Scheduling to do (e.g., half day of work, regular school holiday, make sure there are no doctor appointments that morning, etc.)

_____

_____

List of items to bring:

1. Missals

2. Prayer cards

3. Books for the younger kids

4. _____

5. _____

6. _____

---

[15] Pope Pius XII, *Mediator Dei,* no. 8.

[16] Second Vatican Council, *Sacrosanctum Concilium,* no. 14.

[17] Pope Pius XII, *Mediator Dei,* no. 93. The pope's exact words were that the lay faithful participate at Mass with an "internal worship of the heart."

Chapter 4

Practice and focus

Put yourself in your kids' shoes for a minute. They spend six days a week getting visual and kinesthetic stimulation—*lots* of stimulation. They watch TV, they get shuttled around in moving vehicles, and they play video games. Everything is fast-paced. Everywhere, there is motion, motion, motion.

Then, Sunday comes. Time for Mass.

Where's the constant motion? Where's the great entertaining over-stimulating hyperactivity? Other than a few slow songs, there is no real motion, no shoot-em-up, no knock-em-down, no in-your-face You Want This Now commercials. Life speeds them along at 90 miles an hour all week, and then they're expected to sit still and be quiet during something they don't understand and that bores them half to death. Holy Mass is deep; it is a contemplative thing. It whispers to your brain and sings to your heart. It's hard to change gears from motion-motion-motion and focus on liturgical sobriety.

Do you want to grow closer to our Blessed Lord and Savior? Do you want your children to grow in love and keep their relationship with God?

> Your kids are naughty because they're bored. They are bored because they aren't entertained. They expect entertainment because they've been conditioned to it.

Then teach them about God. Help them focus on His liturgy every Sunday by helping them focus and settle down during the week.

There are two issues with which kids must contend when they attend Mass on Sunday: focus and transition.

Focus

Normal, well-adjusted kids sometimes have trouble focusing on a task in which they are involved. Some children struggle more than others. An entire industry arose in the last decade or so dealing with energetic, unfocused, loud children (usually boys). Boys with mothers who work outside the home. Boys who have mostly female teachers. What's the answer? Label 'em and drug 'em up!

Don't be in a hurry to drug your kids. Research their "disorder" first.

While there is some evidence that Attention-Deficit Hyperactivity Disorder (ADHD) is a real problem and some people really may be helped by treatment, I believe it is one of the most over-diagnosed "disorders" in the nation today. While studying for my undergraduate degree in education, one of my professors surprised me one day when she agreed that the overwhelming majority of ADHD cases are not ADHD at all. It is more a problem of dealing with natural boyhood energy.

I didn't teach in public schools very long, but when I did, I quickly learned methods to focus a classroom of teen and pre-teen kids. A lot of the students were diagnosed as ADHD, and they were on prescription medication. Why didn't anyone notice ADHD a couple hundred years ago? Why is it such

Kids should run. They should run outside. they'll sit still (panting) when you finally let them stop running.

a problem now? Before our modern age, kids didn't have TV, video games, parents with cars, constant boredom, and women who didn't know how to handle them. Back then, they had fathers, lots and lots of farm work, and they walked—everywhere.

Two researchers raised the idea that ADHD could be treated or at least curtailed through proper nutrition. One wrote that children with ADHD could have an iron deficiency,[18] and another simply wrote that proper nutrition seems to help such children.[19] Other researchers make a compelling case that children need to spend a lot more time outdoors—and this will "significantly decrease" ADHD symptoms.[20]

What you can do at home

Focus activities

In my classroom, I discovered a few things that help most children focus on the task at hand. Special-education teachers with whom I worked also used these techniques.

- When your child works on homework or a homeschool assignment, have him sit in a chair properly with both feet under him. Don't let him bury one foot under his knee. You may want to put a notebook or something similar on the ground and have him place both feet on it. This helps him look down at his paper instead of looking around.

- Remind him about his assignment.

- Don't ignore him. Ask how he's doing.

- Set a timer and tell him he must finish. Unfocused children need deadlines. Try a positive approach at first (a reward for finishing before the timer dings) but after a few days, you can resort to punishment or loss of privileges if he still doesn't finish his work.

Some other focusing tips:

- Have your child look down at the paper or whatever it is he or she should focus on.

- Concentrate! Concentrate again. It takes practice.

- Break things down for your child into manageable parts. This particularly helps energetic unfocused children. Instead of handing them a worksheet with twenty problems, use a blank sheet of paper to cover up half the problems. Do the first one for her (but do it slowly and make sure she watches!). Now she only has to focus on nine. Then she can focus on the other ten. Another example from home life: Don't dump a load of clean towels on your nine-year-old son all at once—have him sort the big towels from the washcloths. Then he should fold the big ones, and then the small ones. Now it's three little jobs instead of one overwhelming one.

Finally, the last focusing tip—this may be the most important one. TURN IT OFF! Turn off the noise! No more watching TV, playing video games, or listening to loud, hard-driving music. These things should be the occasional treat, *not* a normal part of a child's daily activities. They should not watch TV every day. You may want music in your house every day, but does it have to be rock music? Try classical music one day, soft rock another day, no music at all the next day, and perhaps light jazz or classical the next. Studies have shown that classical music—compositions from Mozart, Haydn, and Brahms, for example—stimulates the intellectual growth of babies.[21] It will

Unfocused kids are easily overwhelmed.

benefit children of all ages. Rock music, on the other hand, isn't good for anybody. It's just carnal noise.

> Ah! Dearest Lord! I cannot pray,
> My fancy is not free;
> Unmannerly distractions come,
> And force my thoughts from Thee.
>
> The world that looks so dull all day
> Glows bright on me at prayer,
> And plans that ask no thought but then
> Wake up and meet me there.
>
> — Fr. F. Faber: *Distractions in Prayer*
> 19th Century

Turn off the unnecessary noise in your house. At first, you'll need *something* to fill the void—it helps to have good old folk music as well as classical. But after a while, you'll find that silence is golden. If you take away some of the many distractions kids have, they'll be better able to focus. It will work.

"The Lord is not in the wind, the Lord is not in the earthquake, the Lord is not in the fire. The Lord spoke during a whistling of gentle air" (3 Kings 19).

Focusing Worksheet

Which of your children
seem to have more trouble focusing?

Use this worksheet to keep a log of your focusing activities. You can track which activities helped and which didn't seem to make a difference. Use the *Did it help?* section to add comments of your own.

Photocopy this page if you need more worksheets so you have one for each child.

Name of Child _____

Focusing Activity

- Reminders
- Timer set
- Reward (favorite treat, etc)
- Punishment (time out, confiscated toy / privilege, etc.)
- Time alone with no distractions

- Add your own:

_____

_____

_____

_____

_____

Did it help?

_____

_____

_____

_____

Focusing Worksheet

Which of your children
seem to have more trouble focusing?

Use this worksheet to keep a log of your focusing activities. You can track which activities helped and which didn't seem to make a difference. Use the *Did it help?* section to add comments of your own.

Photocopy this page if you need more worksheets so you have one for each child.

Name of Child _____

Focusing Activity

- Reminders
- Timer set
- Reward (favorite treat, etc)
- Punishment (time out, confiscated toy / privilege, etc.)
- Time alone with no distractions

- Add your own:

_____

_____

_____

_____

_____

Did it help?

_____

_____

_____

_____

Focusing Worksheet

Which of your children
seem to have more trouble focusing?

Use this worksheet to keep a log of your focusing activities. You can track which activities helped and which didn't seem to make a difference. Use the *Did it help?* section to add comments of your own.

Photocopy this page if you need more worksheets so you have one for each child.

Name of Child _____

Focusing Activity

• Reminders
• Timer set
• Reward (favorite treat, etc)
• Punishment (time out, confiscated toy / privilege, etc.)
• Time alone with no distractions

• Add your own:

_____

_____

_____

_____

_____

Did it help?

_____

_____

_____

_____

Which of your children
seem to have more trouble focusing?

Use this worksheet to keep a log of your focusing activities. You can track which activities helped and which didn't seem to make a difference. Use the *Did it help?* section to add comments of your own.

Photocopy this page if you need more worksheets so you have one for each child.

Name of Child _____

Focusing Activity

- Reminders
- Timer set
- Reward (favorite treat, etc)
- Punishment (time out, confiscated toy / privilege, etc.)
- Time alone with no distractions

- Add your own:

_____

_____

_____

_____

_____

Did it help?

_____

_____

_____

_____

Role play

Practice attending Mass at home. Your younger kids will love this if you make it a fun game. Set up some chairs or something as a makeshift pew. Have your kids kneel behind the chairs. Begin coaching them, like this:

"Now, what do you do if the child in front of you turns around? (Ignore the errant child and focus on the altar instead.) Little Johnny, show me how you genuflect . . . that's right. What should we do before the gospel? No, use your other thumb."

You get the idea. The kids can take turns being the priest and the altar servers. The nice thing about role-playing at home is that you can speak out loud and give your children practical advice that you simply cannot tell them during a real Mass.

Kids love role playing and stories at bedtime. These can be real teaching moments.

If you need help taking lofty liturgical concepts and presenting them in a format children can understand, fear not. Maria Montessori wrote a book in 1932 that explains the entire traditional Latin Mass to children. This is the same lady who founded the kinesthetic-based Montessori Method of education. The book is entitled *The Mass Explained to Children* and is currently republished by Roman Catholic Books.

"Jesus remains," Montessori wrote,

> thus hidden under the appearance of the Sacrament, which is kept in the locked Tabernacle. So every time a Catholic enters his church he bows down devoutly before Him.... The church is a holy place because of this Real Presence of Jesus.[22]

Now that we've discussed focusing, let's move on to the other issue for your kids: transitioning.

Transition

You race to the church parking lot after driving at highway speeds. Your morning was spent hurrying the kids up. Now, your family is in the church building and Mass will begin soon. If you are like me, you kneel down, take a deep breath, say a few formal prayers like the *Hail Mary*, and then pray informally to God. You are transitioned. The morning rush doesn't matter any longer. However, you are an adult. Your kids can't make the transition that easily. They are in the pew, but their minds are still racing around 90 miles an hour, remembering when they frantically searched for a lost shoe while getting ready for Mass.

They used to say "Godspeed." Now we should say, "Godslow."

A few minutes ago they were rushing along; now they must be quiet and sit still. Transitioning requires practice, and you can practice at home during the week. How?

Structured, consistent family prayer time will really help. For example, every evening at 7:00 PM you can say the rosary together as a family. Or every day before lunch, pray the *Angelus*. Whatever your daily prayer activity, the kids will become used to mentally shifting gears and going from one activity (play time, chores, whatever) to another activity (formal group prayer).

If some of your kids are having a hard time transitioning, coach them during your practice Mass at home during the week. Remind your child when your practice Mass starts that now is the time to focus on the Mass.

"What's happening at the altar, Johnny? Don't worry about (toys, games, whatever). Think about Jesus and Mary now."

You can say these things out loud because you're at home; you can even stand in front of your kids. You aren't stuck in the pew.

Remember, books about the saints really help children during Mass. Kids read them and their minds shift toward whatever they are reading.

empty hands + full minds = fidgety kids

So, spend time during the week on focusing and transitioning activities with your children. Don't let them get on a tangent . . . remind them gently that they should be focusing. If this seems like a lot of work, well . . . it is. But it will pay off quickly. As the weeks go by, two things will happen:

- It will seem easier to do focusing activities because you are used to doing them.

- You will have to do these activities less and less, because your kids are getting better at focusing.

We've touched on the importance of praying together as a family. What else should you as parents do to help your children?

[18] Dr. Bill Sardi, "Is the Primary Cause of Attention Deficit Disorder an Iron Deficiency?" Knowledge of Health, http://www.knowledgeofhealth.com/executelink.asp?story=Is The Primary Cause of Attention Deficit Disorder an Iron Deficiency

[19] Living with ADD, "Tips," http://www.livingwithadd.com/tips.shtml

[20] Frances E. Kuo, Ph.D., "A Potential Natural Treatment for Attention-Deficit/ Hyperactivity Disorder," American Journal of Public Health, Sept. 2004 (online at http://www.ajph.org/cgi/content/full/94/9/1580) para. 25.

[21] Denise Winterman, "Does Classical Music Make Babies Smarter?" BBC News, May 19, 2005: http://news.bbc.co.uk/2/hi/uk_news/magazine/4558507.stm

[22] Maria Montessori, *The Mass Explained to Children* (Fort Collins, CO: Roman Catholic Books, orig. pub. 1932) p. 9.

Chapter 5

The parent's role

Stability!

If you want to build a great tower, you plan it first with blueprints, then use good building materials, and finally put it all together. But what if the foundation is weak? What good are the strongest metal and the best hardware if the ground is swampy? The tower simply will not be good enough to stand tall, no matter how well built.

You are really trying to raise up well-behaved children who will lead good, moral lives, frequent the sacraments, and strengthen their relationships with Jesus Christ. But what about you and your spouse? Are your lives stable? The stability and security of the parents are the foundation for good behavior at Mass. If children are being shuttled from one separated parent to another, or if their father is in prison, or their grandparents undermine parental authority, or the children are moved to a new home every year, you cannot expect much good behavior from them.

First, fix their home life. This is key; this is the foundation upon which you will build good behavior. Children act out when they are not secure.

Kids from broken homes learn that life is unstable and people are untrustworthy. They behave accordingly, whether in the classroom, their own house, the group home, or the church building.

If your family is experiencing some unstable circumstances, you can still try some of the strategies outlined in this book, but to be honest, you will only meet limited success. Focus your efforts on the roots of the instability. Is it fixable, or is this a permanent situation? Can the problems at least be curtailed for a while?

Everyone goes through temporary events that shake the stability of the family—a move across town, a new job, whatever—so the important thing is for the parents to remain calm and be as secure as they can for the children. Do not discuss upsetting things in front of the children until you and your spouse find a solution. *Then* talk to the kids about it if needed.

The family may be regarded as the cradle of civil society, and it is in great measure within the circle of family life that the destiny of states is fostered.
— Pope Leo XIII: *Sapientiae Christianae*
January 10, 1890

You can dramatically improve your Catholic home life's stability and organization in the next twelve months. For starters, make a rough daily schedule and stick with it. Another thing modern families seem to have a lot of trouble with is getting the kids to bed on time. This is essential! They behave a lot better if they aren't tired.

You may notice that some (or all) of your kids respond better to structure and stability than others. These children will be better behaved if you attend the same church or chapel every Sunday. It's one thing to jump around to a different parish for a few weeks until you settle down in a solid parish, but don't make a habit of it. There is a spiritual benefit to staying in one place, for both adults and children.

Kids from stable homes aren't always "perfect angels," but they don't have any deep, compelling reasons for bad behavior.

"He can't help it—he was born that way"

What if you've tried to make your children behave, but nothing seems to work? What if one or two of your children are particularly stubborn? Could they have been born that way? Is there anything you can do about that?

In psychology—especially the "behavioral" and "psychoanalytical" schools—there is a long-running debate over "nature" vs. "nurture." In other words, do human beings behave the way they do because they were *born* that way (genetic, biological determination) or because they were *raised* that way by their parents and their surrounding environment? A common-sense reaction would seem to be: both, to some degree. The choleric child can be especially stubborn and is wired that way from birth. But let's take a closer look at the debate.

What motivates psychologists and their patients to find the cause of one's behavior? Why do they want to know? Is it to help the individual avoid sin, live a moral life, and work on character imperfections? Or is it is to feel better about one's immoral behavior, without changing it? The late doctor Rudolph Allers, an early 20th century Catholic psychologist, had strong opinions about the nature (heredity) vs. nurture (environment) debate.

> There is, however, a special reason why the theory that character is due exclusively to heredity has met such an approval and why it is not discarded, though it is evidently disproved by facts. The idea that character is determined by the inexorable laws of heredity supplies in fact an all too welcome pretext for not attempting any change. Laziness and unwillingness for strenuous action finds an apparently valid excuse in this theory. It is indeed more pleasant to imagine

character and personality as beyond the reach of human will and of human exertion.[23]

Doctor Allers then draws a conclusion to his findings:

> It is surely easier to think that one can not help being what one is, than to know that one could be different if only one would endeavor earnestly enough. This is probably the strongest reason for the approval the theory of heredity has met. . . . To see this attitude justified by 'science' is surely a great consolation.[24]

Doctor Allers penned those words almost 70 years ago, before the word processor was invented. Now, fast forward to the 21st century. The web site for the PBS TV show NOVA featured an article titled "Nature vs Nurture Revisited." The article is part of the show's "Cracking the Code of Life" series, produced when scientists were working on the human genome project. One of the researchers came to the same conclusion Doctor Allers reached back in the 1930s.

> After a decade of hype surrounding the Human Genome Project, punctuated at regular intervals by gaudy headlines proclaiming the discovery of genes for killer diseases and complex traits, this unexpected result led some journalists to a stunning conclusion. The seesaw struggle between our genes—nature—and the environment—nurture—had swung sharply in favor of nurture. 'We simply do not have enough genes for this idea of biological determinism to be right,' asserted Craig Venter, president of Celera Genomics, one of the two teams that cracked the human genome.[25]

The conclusion? Don't believe for a minute that your stubborn little Billy cannot behave at Mass because he was "born that way." *You and your spouse* can shape his behavior, regardless of his temperament. You can do it, with God's help. Why not pray to the troublesome child's guardian angel?

> Stubbornness is a perceived vice in children, but it can be a virtue. Little Billy is stubborn about candy today; twenty years from now, Bill can stubbornly resist temptation.

Unless your child has moderate retardation, you can change his behavior using the strategies outlined in this little book. Notice I didn't use the phrase "learning disability." Learning-disabled children can exhibit just as good or bad behavior as children who have no trouble learning new concepts. Even moderately slow children can be directed to some degree. Pray to their guardian angels!

This isn't to say that a birth defect cannot affect one's behavior. It happens, but that is a rare situation. Practically all the emotional and behavioral problems of both children and adults stem from their own choices in life or their reactions to the way they were raised.

All dressed up

We discussed stability and your role in nurturing good children. Now let's consider their attire. Your children simply *must* wear their Sunday best for Mass. If they don't dress differently for Mass, can you expect them to behave differently? Holy Mass is an important event; remember, it is Redemption itself, applied for us today. Dress up!

Besides the Mass, let's discuss clothing in general for a moment. Ladies, how do you feel in a jogging suit? Now, how do you feel in an evening gown with jewelry? Gentlemen, would you show

> "Clothes make the man."
> — Mark Twain

up for a business meeting in shorts and sandals if your boss and an important client were there? Probably not! You dress appropriately for the occasion.

The clothing we wear matters. Clothing changes our behavior; it changes how people feel; it certainly changes what people think of you, especially in a first impression. One columnist advocates dressing up on a regular basis whenever one must go out in public.

> Elevated dressing causes people to behave better. Crime might fall. Manners would begin to come back. People might clean up their language. They might listen to better music and read better books. Something resembling civilization might return.[26]

Many universities have entire programs of study on human ecology or human behavior and the textiles industry. Oregon State University's Department of Design and Human Environment has graduate-level courses in their "Emphasis in Clothing" concentration, such as "DHE 677: Theoretical Frameworks in Fashion" and "DHE 577: Fashion Theory."[27] The University of Wisconsin-Madison has a "Textiles Specialization" under the School of Human Ecology.[28] This is serious stuff, folks. Clothing affects your behavior.

Children should never be taken to church in a dress which would not be thought good enough for appearing before company.
— St. John Baptist de la Salle: *The Rules of Christian Manners and Civility*, 3.
17th Century

Sunday attire is not only respectful toward God (after all, you are visiting His house), the clothing actually helps to orient the child's mind toward the liturgy. Something different is happening, the child thinks, something special. Today is Sunday. I'm wearing my Sunday clothes, not my play clothes.

Do you love your spouse? Do you dress up for a night out? If you dress up for your husband or wife, shouldn't you also dress up when you visit God's house, if you say you love Him?

You are setting up the child to think about Mass even when he gets dressed Sunday morning.

Your Sunday best

Ladies, consider wearing a skirt or dress to Mass that covers your knees while you are sitting. Men, the minimum—minimum!—that you should wear to Sunday Mass are semi-casual slacks and a shirt with buttons. A long-sleeved dress shirt and tie is better. Wear a jacket and tie if you can.

You read earlier all the reasons your *children* need to dress up for Mass. The same reasons apply to us adults: respect for God, orienting our minds toward the liturgy because we are dressed differently, and being part of the refinement of civilization. For parents, there's another reason: providing a good example for your kids.

Kids are influenced by their teachers, their peers, TV, music, and advertising. But their biggest influence is still . . . . you.

Be a good example!

The child thinks: If Mommy and Daddy dress up for Mass, then I should, too. It must be important. If Mommy and Daddy take Mass seriously, it must be important. If Mommy covers her knees when she sits in the pew, then I have to sit like a little lady. If Daddy never puts his foot up on the kneeler in front of him while he sits, I shouldn't either.

If Daddy goes to Holy Communion and prays for a long time afterward, then it must be important. If Mommy and Daddy don't eat before Holy Communion, it must be really important, 'cause I know Mommy loves to eat!

If Mommy and Daddy are quiet in church and say the prayers during Mass and they stay afterward to say more prayers, it must be important. My Mommy and Daddy are teaching me because of what they *do,* not only what they *say.*

Like father, like son: every good tree maketh good fruits.
— Wm. Langland: *Piers Plowman,* 3.
    14th Century

Someday, your children will outgrow their chronic need for your help, your clothing them, your feeding them, and even your money. Everyone talks about this.

"They grow up so fast."

"When he was little, he would talk non-stop. Now he never says a word to me."

And so on. But when you grow *away* from something, you also grow *toward* something else. As your children grow up and they need parental care less and less, they should be growing toward Jesus Christ. That is the whole point of saving one's soul. They will grow toward something—money, bad friends, materialism, hedonism, whatever—so help them grow in their relationship with God instead.

You have the saints on your side when you instill virtue in your kids. Many of the saints wrote about perseverance and family life. "God does not command impossibilities," wrote Saint Augustine, "but by commanding admonishes you to do what you can and to pray for what you cannot, and aids you that you may be able."[29]

What do you think your kids will be like when they're grown up?

Use this space to list each of your children's names and write your thoughts about their future.

Child's Name: as ⬤ adult:	Character Traits/Behaviors
⬤	
⬤	
⬤	
⬤	
⬤	
⬤	
⬤	

"Perfect married life," wrote the wise Saint Thomas Aquinas, "means the complete dedication of the parents for the benefit of their children."[30] Not exactly modern thinking, is it?

Saint John Vianney, known as the Curé of Ars, was a parish priest in France. He saw the utter moral and cultural devastation of the French Revolution, and knew the key to rebuilding civilization. This man is one of the greatest saints in the Church. He spent hours each day in the confessional, and hours in prayer before God!

"The reason why our times are so irreligious," the Curé of Ars said, "is on account of the unchristian families. Where the wrong was, there must be the remedy. All the authority of Church and State is useless if the family does not co-operate."[31]

Learning to love the Mass

Many times, parents are found exclaiming, "He was so cute when he was little and said his prayers. But now that he's twenty-something, he never goes to church!" The child learned that Mass, Catholic spirituality, and the sacraments are important to his parents. That's all. He never learned to love these things *on his own.* He went to Mass as a child because his parents insisted; now he is a young adult, and he puts it aside because he views it as childish. Mass is what the *parents* want, but it's not what the adult child wants. If he is experimenting with ideas and rejects the values of his parents, he will reject Sunday Mass attendance.

Adolescents need adult Catholic role models outside their immediate family, and devout Catholic friends. Without them, the young adult may stop attending Mass.

Talk about throwing out the baby with the bathwater.

Young adults are supposed to learn and sort out ideas themselves. They should have intellectual conversations with their parents, grandparents, and others who are older than themselves.[32] But this intellectual growth should be toward God and the liturgy, not away from it.

Instill a love of our Eucharistic Lord now, when your children are still under your care. Teach them by word and example that the little Host really is Jesus, Who becomes Food for our soul. Remind them that adults go to Holy Communion as well as children. Our Lord loves your children and He wants them to go to Heaven. They need to learn as they become adolescents that it's manly (or lady-like) to have a relationship with Christ. Hopefully they will have good friends and older role models at their parish; that will help keep them there. As the early and outstanding Catholic psychiatrist, Doctor Rudolf Allers, wrote in one of his books,

> ...we see quite frequently the very same youngsters who revolt against some traditional authority (of parents, of teachers, or of the Church) astonishingly ready to submit to some other authority.[33]

Show them that their sacramental relationship with Jesus and Mary is a separate thing from their relationship with their parents.

A priest once told me of a mother who took the utmost care in preparing her little boy for his First Holy Communion. She taught him; she went over prayers with him; she took him to catechism lessons. She fretted and helped him with his Holy Communion outfit that Sunday morning. Imagine how happy our Lord Jesus was when He finally rested on the tongue and into the heart of that innocent boy! It was a beautiful day and the boy said his prayers after Mass. He was developing a love of our Lord in the Holy Eucharist.

That afternoon, the boy's father took him aside and said, "You don't really believe all that garbage about Communion, do you?" Remember, this is a little boy. He naturally looks up to his father. Of course, the boy told his father no, he didn't believe it. He wanted to be just like his dad.

In that moment, a blossoming relationship with Jesus Christ was smashed into the ground.

---

[23] Rudolph Allers, M.D., Ph.D., *Self Improvement* (Fort Collins, CO: Roman Catholic Books, orig. pub. 1938) p. 57.

[24] Ibid.

[25] Kevin Davies, "Nature vs Nurture Revisited" (NOVA Online: "Cracking the Code of Life," PBS.org) para. 2. From http://www.pbs.org/wgbh/nova/genome/debate.html.

[26] Jeffrey Tucker, "How to Dress Like a Man," LewRockwell.Com, July 16, 2003, http://www.lewrockwell.com/tucker/tucker38.html

[27] Oregon State University, College of Health & Human Sciences, Graduate Studies, http://www.hhs.oregonstate.edu/dhe/graduate/clothing-human-behavior.html

[28] University of Wisconsin-Madison, Graduate School Catalog 2006–2008, Human Ecology, http://www.wisc.edu/grad/catalog/sohe/sohe.html

[29] Johnston, *Voice*, p. 102.

[30] Ibid.

[31] Ibid., p. 105.

[32] *Integrity: Raising Your Children* (Kansas City, MO: Angelus Press, 1995) pp. 9–10.

[33] Rudolph Allers, M.D., Ph.D., *Forming Character in Adolescents* (Fort Collins, CO: Roman Catholic Books, originally published 1940) p. 64.

Chapter 6

Things that help—and things that hurt

The joy of eating

Should you feed your children breakfast before Sunday Mass? You probably have a gut feeling that somehow, you and your family should follow the midnight fast—no food from midnight until after Holy Communion Sunday morning. Or perhaps you follow the three-hour fast instituted by Pope Pius XII. But what about little kids? What if your daughter is only nine-years old? As a practical matter, do you have time to make your kids breakfast while getting ready for Mass?

Generally, kids behave better when they have full tummies. But that also makes them more awake and alert; they can focus better, but they're more fidgety. What to do?

You may want to consider feeding your preschoolers and toddlers before Mass. It's pretty hard for them to endure without eating. If you're home with them during the week, you also know if someone is having a growth spurt and needs more food. As I wrote earlier, you can give the little ones breakfast bars, cheese sticks, Pop Tarts, or something without sugar, in the car on the way to church. You can also try hard-boiled eggs and bags of dry cereal. Explain the idea of fasting to the

Fasting and purity go hand in hand. The first is spiritual ammunition in the fight to preserve the second. Fasting is a form of self-mortification, which trains the will to resist impurity.

older ones. A healthy seven- or eight-year-old can certainly do a three-hour fast.

The key word there is "healthy." This doesn't apply if your kid is skinny as a bean pole, has the flu, was awake twice in the middle of the night, and hadn't eaten since 6:30 PM the night before. The combination of these factors will probably make him literally faint in the pew during the Offertory no matter how old he is. Give this child a granola bar before Mass. Better yet—keep him home and have your spouse bring the healthy ones to church.

Subdue your flesh by fasting and abstinence from meat and drink, as far as the health allows.
— St. Augustine: *Letter 211* (his Rule).
   5th Century

> Fasting is a medicine.
> — St. John Chrysostom: *Homilies.*
>   4th Century

You can also try what some families do: No one eats. Dress the kids in their church clothes the night before, wake up an hour before Mass, load everyone in the car and drive over there. They may look a little wrinkled and by the time they really wake up (usually during the gospel), they start to get hungry, but it generally works for younger children.

Proper nutrition

Food affects behavior. If your children eat a typical American diet, change it. Cut back on the refined sugary stuff and gradually increase their vegetables, meats, and cheeses during the week. (If it comes in a box or a wrapper, it's refined sugary stuff. If it's a whole food item that someone actually has to cut up and

Don't accept the government food pyramid schemes at face value. Do your own research on food and nutrition.

cook, it's good for you.) There is a lot of debate over the link between sugar and behavior, so try different foods and see if you notice any changes. At the time of this writing, there was a lot of conflicting information on the Internet about sugar and its effects on behavior, so the best advice is this: use trial and error. Cut back on white sugar and see if it makes a difference in your own body.

These events are beyond our control

If your kids are sick or going through something stressful (like a house move or grandparent's death) they will not be as well-behaved during Mass that week. There is nothing you can do about that. If they are overly tired, they will not behave as well either. When you arrive at the church, there won't be anything you can do about it. What can you do next week to make the liturgy go better for you?

Go to bed early next Saturday night. You may want to get them outside on Saturday so they get a lot of fresh air, and sleep more soundly.

Setting the standard

As a parent, you need to be fair with your kids. Expect the same behavior from all of them. The well-known Catholic priest and author, the late Father Paul Wickens, said that reluctance to consistently exercise parental authority is the main fault of modern parents.[34] Be consistent and don't let one child wear you down when you already told another child "no" about the same thing. Steady, fair discipline will reap stable, obedient children. They will still push your limits and test you, but they expect you to have boundaries! Make sure you are disciplining them for their sake, not because you are finally annoyed with them.

Don't play favorites with your children. Give each one some individual time and attention, and they'll be happy. So will you.

A note on single mothers

You can see that having two parents in the pew is a good strategy. But what if you're a single mother? Or what if your spouse doesn't attend Mass with you?

You may be able to get another relative to help you. What about a grandfather or an uncle? The male relative does not have to be a "strict disciplinarian"; this doesn't usually occur with grandchildren or nieces and nephews anyway. But the mere presence of a trusted male relative in the middle of the pew is enough to moderate your children's behavior. The uncle or grandparent can help direct the children's attention to the altar.

So far, we've discussed the importance of focusing, nutrition, the role of parents, and eating before Mass. We can see that consistent parental authority is important, but how does that really work in the real world of diapers, sandwiches, and video games? What about spankings? How much discipline is too much? What if you have teenagers? Read the next chapter to get answers to these and more.

---

[34] Fr. Paul Wickens, *Handbook for Parents* (Long Prairie, MN: The Neumann Press, 1987) p. 15.

Chapter 7

The final word—discipline!

Do not be afraid to discipline your children. Kids will try all kinds of ways to manipulate you, and they will play the parents against each other. Don't fall for it. Yes means yes and no means no. If it wasn't ok to eat candy before bedtime a week ago, it isn't ok tonight. If sweet-hearted Sally bites rough-and-tumble Billy, she needs a light tap on the face or perhaps a spanking on her bottom. She needs to be corrected, or she won't be sweet-hearted for long.

Parents have a natural tendency to want good things for their children. This is good. But too often it translates into a reluctance to go against the strong will of a child, even when the discipline is clearly needed. As Father Wickens wrote,

> Because children do not always know what is best for them, adults have an obligation to act in their best interest, whether the children like it or not. (e.g., Take them to the dentist, make them do homework, turn off the T.V., say their prayers, attend Mass on Sunday.)[35]

The entire history of the Western world, until the twentieth century, shows an overwhelming approval of strict and firm discipline of children. The late philosopher, Doctor Mortimer Adler, wrote that, "practically all the great writers insist that parents should govern children firmly until they reach maturity."[36] Doctor Adler presented examples (not necessarily Catholic) ranging from Aristotle in pre-Christian times, Locke from the 17th Century, and even Freud from more recent times. All these men recognized that "parents rule the child in order to fit him for adult freedom."[37] Freud, who taught that strict parental rule can harm children, also taught "leniency and indulgence may have just as bad emotional effects as harshness and strictness."[38] Freud's ideas on child development and his theory of psychoanalysis have serious flaws. But isn't it interesting—even someone without a solid Christian concept of the nature of man, like Freud, recognized that leniency can harm the development of children!

Doctor Adler summed up traditional Western thinking by writing, "Parental rule is tyrannical and unjust only when the parents are concerned with their own power and ease, or extend their rule beyond adolescence."[39]

Set firm and loving limits. Kids crave boundaries and stability.

In the 1830s, the War Between the States hadn't yet begun. The United States was still a young nation of states and territories, and the telegraph and telephone hadn't been invented. The Revolutionary War and the War of 1812 were still recent memories. Yet, early Americans knew that firm discipline in childhood, coupled with tenderness and attention from both mother and father, brought about well-adjusted young adults.

If you want to make the world a better place to live, don't look to the future for answers. Look to what worked in the past.

A cursory look at literature from that era, even Protestant literature, reveals that they had some of the same problems as we do, except there were relatively few bad parents back then, mostly confined to the poorer classes. Today, bad parenting is so widespread it is considered "normal." A Presbyterian minister from Philadelphia wrote in 1838 that,

We often visit houses where the parents seem to be mere advisory attendants, with a painful sinecure. Let such hear the words of a wise Congressman of New Jersey, and a signer of the Declaration: 'There is not a more disgusting sight than the impotent rage of a parent who has no authority. Among the lower ranks of people, who are under no restraints from decency, you may sometimes see a father or mother running out into the street after a child who has fled from them, with looks of fury and words of execration; and they are often stupid enough to imagine that neighbours or passengers will approve them in their conduct, though in fact it fills every beholder with horror.'[40]

The minister then shocked his readers with a story of a very small child who innocently walked in front of a moving train, and just missed being run over. The child's mother emerged from the door of a "low shanty," when

> [T]he sturdy mother, more full of anger than alarm, strode forth, and seizing the poor infant, which had strayed only in consequence of her own negligence, gave it a summary and violent correction . . . . Inference: parents often deserve the strokes they give.[41]

Immediate obedience, the minister wrote, should be insisted upon very early in a child's life. This will pave the way so that later, there will not be much need of spankings: "It holds universally in families and schools, and even the greater bodies of men, the army and navy, that those who keep the strictest discipline give the fewest strokes."

Children focus better when the room is quiet and strict order is enforced.

But what of parental attention, to add balance to the strictness? The same minister wrote—remember, this was in 1838!—the following, which I will quote at length.

> Here is a man who drives his children out of his shop, because they pester him; here is another who is always too busy to give them a good word. Now I would gladly learn of these penny-wise and pound-foolish fathers, what work they expect ever to turn out, which shall equal in importance the children who are now taking their mould for life. Hapless is that child which is forced to seek for companions more accessible and winning than its father or its mother.
>
> You may observe that when a working man spends his leisure hours *abroad,* it is at the expense of his family. While he is at the club or the tavern, his boy or girl is seeking out-of-door connexions. The great school of juvenile vice is the *street.* Here the urchin ... learns the vulgar oath, or the putrid obscenity. For one lesson at the fireside, he has a dozen in the kennel.
>
> Love home yourself; sink your roots deeply among your domestic treasures; set an example in this . . . The garden-plant seems to have accomplished its great work, and is content to wither, when it has matured the fruit for the next race: learn a lesson from the plant.[42]

Your discipline will be much, much more effective if you are actually around for your kids to see you—especially as they get older. If they only see you once in a while, they might fear you, but they won't have as much respect.

You have to set boundaries. Think of your parental boundaries as a block fence or a concrete wall. It is unmovable.

No matter the circumstances, no matter which child goes against that boundary wall, the boundaries are the same. You must be consistent. You may also think of your boundaries as a swaying palm tree that stands firm, but will accommodate within reason if it turns out the parent is wrong. If you discover that you were incorrect about something, there is no need to continue saying "no" to a child simply to retain authority.

Let's play the Authority Scale game!

Where are you on the scale?

When your child asks you for something again after you say "no," which object most represents your ability to stand firm?

Rock—unmovable.

Palm tree—bends a little in the wind, but it stands tall and won't fall over.

Clay—can be molded with a little pressure.

Marshmallow—need we say more?

Be honest with yourself and circle the most accurate object!

Wife	Husband
rock	rock
palm tree	palm tree
clay	clay
marshmallow	marshmallow

Notes: _____

_____

_____

_____

There was a time in our household when some of the kids would ask the other parent for something when the first parent said no.

"Mommy, can I play outside?"

"No, because it's almost dinner time and you still haven't picked up your toys."

The child walks to the other room, where the oblivious father sits engrossed in a newspaper.

"Daddy, can I play outside?"

"Sure, kiddo!"

Before long, my wife and I agreed to answer every single question with a question: did you ask your mother / did you ask your father already? The kids would actually get in trouble if they asked the other parent the same question after receiving an answer they didn't want to hear. The manipulation stopped. *Et erunt duo in carne una.* Indeed, "they two shall be in one flesh" (St. Matthew 19:5).

Present a united front to your children, and they will better understand authority.

From where does authority come? It comes from God. The children need to understand this as they grow older and become adolescents. Authority does not come *from* Mom or Dad, it comes *through* them. The root of the word "discipline" means to bring order necessary for instruction. To correct, to train, to instruct: That's what discipline is really all about! Discipline is correction for the good of the child. It is not necessarily punishment so that Mommy and Daddy feel better after the child is naughty (although sometimes that is a side benefit).

Christ is the bridegroom; the Catholic Church is the bride. You and your spouse must be likewise united. Never contradict each other in front of the kids.

When you need to discipline one of your children, do it for their sake, not for your convenience. Don't wait until *you* are irritated by his behavior to discipline him. Your children will incorrectly learn as they get older that Mom or Dad is the one from whom authority comes. Teach them that true authority comes from God; He is the One to whom they should turn. The flip side of that coin is that children should be loved and accepted because they are gifts from God, not because you need them or because they make you feel special. Young adults who experienced this parental "love" may become neurotic. Saint Catherine of Siena said that "children should be loved for the love of Him who created them, and not for the love of self nor of the children."[43]

When my wife manages our children during the day, the kids get in trouble if they don't do their duties. Sometimes, when she has to make the children do unpleasant things (Math! Yuck!), she reminds them that *she* will get in trouble with God if she doesn't raise them correctly. The kids are awed at such a responsibility. They still don't like math, or chores, or picking up toys, but her strategy usually works.

Babies are beautiful

The laughter of toddlers and small children is a joy to hear. But if they sense their worth comes from their beauty or their behavior, they'll feel too much pressure as they grow up. Teach them that God loves them exactly as they are and He has a plan for them. They should also sense your strong, consistent love for them, regardless of what they look like or how they act. You may feel *disappointed* in bad behavior, but you still *love* them. The result is normal, well-adjusted adults.

Teenagers

A lot of what I've covered so far deals with younger children. But what about teenagers? If you haven't expected good behavior from them all along, it will be more difficult to start now that they are teens.

Drill sergeants and shooting instructors tell the following scenario to their students. It illustrates a planning strategy.

Question: *Let's say you are in a dark alley at night. Three thugs walk up to you, and two of them reach behind their backs. What do you do?*

Answer: *What were you doing there in the first place?*

A personal example will also illustrate this. One night I was really tired. Well, I was being lazy. The garbage was full and needed to be taken out. We lived in a drafty old house, and it was the middle of summer, and there were lots of insects outside. I decided to leave the garbage and take it out in the morning.

I awoke the next morning, stretched my arms, and stumbled my way into the kitchen.

Ants!

Hundreds of ants. Ants in a neat assembly line, marching across the kitchen floor, swarming up and down the garbage can. Ugh! I wanted to rewind my life and go back to the night before. Where's a time machine when you need one?

The same principles apply to raising children. It's a lot easier if you discipline them from the time they're in training pants. Then, when they're teenagers, they'll kneel, sit, and stand appropriately for Mass, and they may even get something out of it.

Older kids who exhibit rude or noisy behavior might not know how to behave. They've never been properly trained.

Let's say you've had an epiphany moment while reading this workbook, and you want to instill discipline and good behavior in your teenagers from this point forward. Great! You are to be congratulated for taking your role as a Catholic parent more seriously. It's like when I sincerely repented of eating cheesecake. I am heartily sorry for having eaten cheesecake, and I promise to avoid the near occasions of cheesecake. But hey! I still have a generous pot belly. I decided to eat healthier, but the effects of my former behavior still show. Gee, this will take—*hard work!*

It will take a bit of work to re-train your older children to behave differently than they have been. But fear not: it can be done. You must be consistent, and you also have to *clearly explain why* you are changing your expectations. You don't have to clarify anything to your four-year-old, but you should talk to your fourteen-year-old about the Mass. Appeal to his ability to reason.[44]

> Natural reason is a good tree which God has planted in us;
> the fruits which spring from it cannot but be good.
> — St. Francis de Sales: *Treatise on the Love of God,* II, I.
> 17th Century

When you tell your teenagers about the Mass and why, from now on, the family will absolutely behave in the pew, do not argue with them. This isn't so much a *discussion* as it is an *explanation.* They deserve to be told the reasons why they must behave better at Mass and not have lazy-butt syndrome, but don't let them talk back. Questions from them are definitely ok, but do not bargain with them.

Remember, teens appreciate stability just as little kids do. Teenagers *need* stability and security; they need you to establish standards of behavior for them at Holy Mass.

Teens believe something is really important when both parents discuss a topic with them.

The father's role at this point is critical. For some reason, teenage boys tune out their mothers. Home schooling Moms begin to notice that their thirteen-year-old sons aren't as easy to work with as they were a year earlier. When a mother lectures her teenage son, he gets glassy-eyed. The teens tend to respond better to their father. The father of the family must be a significant part of the "good behavior at Mass" lessons for teens.

Don't be afraid to tell your teens that you are adjusting your expectations of them during Holy Mass. Yes, they will interpret this to mean you made a mistake in the past or did something wrong, and now you're trying to fix it. Well, they are basically correct. But this is a normal part of parenting. As Doctor Allers put it,

> ...an open avowal of an error does not diminish authority; it even strengthens the bond between child and parents, because their relation thus becomes, so to say, more human. Although the belief in the parents' infallibility disappears, something more valuable is gained. The intellectual authority, if one may express it in this way, becomes less, but the moral authority grows.[45]

In the lives of Christians we look not to the beginnings but to the endings.
— St. Jerome: *Letters*, 54,6.
  4th Century

A bump on a log

Sometimes, your teens will sit during Mass with their arms crossed, and getting them to kneel is like raising the Titanic. They just sit there and get nothing out of the liturgy. There isn't much you can *physically* do about that. Your adolescent needs a change of heart. However, this isn't as hard as it sounds. They are very impressionable. What if their friends at school are not Catholic? What if their friends at your parish also sit there like bumps on a log?

Teens respond to their environment. If your teen is surrounded by devout teens, he will be devout. If he is surrounded by worldly agnostics, he will be worldly and doubt the existence of God. When I worked at a high school for "academically challenged" youth, there was a group of about five boys with very nasty attitudes. None of them learned anything in any of the classrooms and they were all disruptive to some degree, depending upon the teacher. Eventually, most of them either dropped out or were expelled. There was one boy left from that original group. Around the same time, the school also changed its focus. Administrators tightened the rules and began actively recruiting smarter kids. Academics became more rigorous. The boy responded very well to his new environment. One day, he actually apologized to me for his former behavior in my classroom.

Teens can change. But it takes time, a favorable environment, and prayer on your part. Pray for your children. Change their

As long as your adolescent children live at home, you can still make a positive impression on them.

environment if you can. If your daughter is a public school senior graduating in four months, and she isn't miserable at school, you may as well let her finish her classes there. But otherwise, it's not too late to move your children to a Catholic school.

Give them time to change. Oftentimes, they slouch in the pew with their arms crossed simply because they see other teens sitting the same way. Peer pressure is unbelievably powerful. This is why it's so important to raise them in a favorable environment.

You can also appeal to their desire to be grown up. Tell your teens you need their help, and you'd like them to show the younger children in the family how to sit, kneel, and stand the correct way. Tell your teenaged son or daughter that you need them to be a good example, since the teen is so much older than the younger children. You might be surprised at how well your teens respond to this strategy. You are directly appealing to their desire for older responsibilities and adult privileges.

Argumentum ad grown-upum: A logical fallacy that happens when teenagers crave more privileges and less acne.

PRACTICAL DISCIPLINE

Corporal punishment

Are spankings okay? Of course they are! See all those nasty-looking teenagers in the mall? The ones with earrings all over their bodies, dressed in black, with messy hair and long faces? Half of them were never spanked, and the other half were hit too much—when they were too old to be hit—and for the wrong reasons.

Little children should be spanked for infractions after a warning. By the age of five, the spankings should naturally occur less and less. By the time the child is about eight-years-old, they shouldn't need any more spankings. Take privileges away instead, or make them stand in a "time-out" corner of your house. (*Warning:* over time, the paint and drywall of this corner will look noticeably dirtier than the rest of your house).

This is very general advice. It is the very rare child, usually the lazy phlegmatic male who is not very observant of external situations, who can be spanked all the way into junior high. Even then, the spankings will be seldom. They are more effective for these older boys when the spankings are rare.

Doctor James Dobson,

You have an impulse to spank naughty children. Go with that — but do it for their correction, not from your anger.

the popular psychologist, wrote that spankings should only be administered for "deliberate disobedience or defiance." Doctor Dobson also recommends giving your child a firm warning first, if you cannot tell whether his action was deliberate or not.[46]

When and where to spank

Don't spank your three-year-old in the grocery store. If she is naughty, you may have to leave the cart and take her outside or to the car. Better yet, duck into a section of the store that isn't used very much, and speak directly to her. Remind her that if she doesn't stop crying/pouting/playing with the produce, that she will be spanked when you leave the store.

For the same reason, don't spank your child in the pew at Mass. Not very hard, anyway. It is not advisable to cause a scene and draw attention to yourself. Publicly embarrassing your children is not a good strategy; it could cause problems in your children later in life. Private correction is best, particularly for girls.

When you spank, spank their bottoms. Don't hit their head or slap their faces if they are disobedient or cruel to others. If they stick out their tongues, bite someone, or use bad language, then you can *lightly* give them a tap on the cheek.

Spank bottoms for disobedience after a warning. Tap cheeks for using their mouths or words inappropriately.

I mentioned spanking in the pew. After a warning, you can lightly but firmly slap their bottoms in the pew. This is a reminder to them that they will get a harder spanking outside the church building if they don't behave right now. Use discretion because you don't want to cause your four-year-old to start crying out loud when everyone around you is kneeling in silence.

Recently, my six-year-old son was not kneeling correctly in his pew. I gave him a warning. Ten seconds later, his laziness began again. He received a second warning and my hand touched his arm. Five seconds later, he was leaning on the pew in front of him yet again, with arms dangling down and one foot stretched out beyond his pew space. I was really tired; I had four small kids to watch while my wife held the baby, and I had enough distractions during Mass without having to deal with this kid. I became increasingly agitated.

What I wanted to do:

Pick up the six-year-old, aim toward the middle aisle, and throw him out of the pew. Push all the other kids away from me and bury my face in my Missal.

What I actually did:

I whispered, "If you don't kneel straight, you won't get a doughnut after Mass. Do you want a doughnut? Then straighten up right now!"

Problem solved.

[35] Wickens, *Handbook,* 15.

[36] Mortimer Adler, *Great Ideas from the Great Books* (New York: Washington Square Press, 1963) p. 193.

[37] Ibid., p. 194.

[38] Ibid., p. 195.

[39] Ibid., pp. 194–195.

[40] Carl Bode, ed., *American Life in the 1840s* (New York: Anchor Books, 1967) pp. 80–81.

[41] Ibid., p. 81.

[42] Ibid., p. 82. Emphasis in original.

[43] Johnston, *Voice,* p. 104.

[44] Allers, *Character,* p. 70.

[45] Ibid., pp. 70–71.

[46] James Dobson, *The Strong-Willed Child* (Wheaton, IL: Tyndale House Publishing, Inc., 1985), pp. 87–88.

Chapter 8

Week by week training plan

The first week

1. Offer up your behavior strategy to God. Pick a patron saint for your behavior project. Invoke the Blessed Virgin Mary, Saint John Vianney, Saint John Bosco, Ven. Anna Maria Taigi, Saint Joseph, or Saint Thomas More. You need help. Don't go it alone.

2. Tell the kids that you are changing your expectations of them. Warn them that they will have to sit, stand, and kneel quietly during Sunday Mass from now on. Discussing this during the week will help.

3. Spend two days this week, just a few minutes each day, talking about the Mass and telling them why they must behave. The church is God's house. We show Him respect by behaving well and not distracting others. Practice genuflecting.

4. Plan your sitting strategy with your spouse. Who will sit where? Which pew should we try to take?

5. Offer more prayers for the intention of having better-behaved kids during Holy Mass. Ask God to help you. Ask Saint Thomas More to intercede for you; he had noisy kids.

6. It's Saturday night! Go to bed early.

Notes on our pew strategy

_____

_____

_____

_____

7. Sunday morning: Feed the toddlers a light breakfast. Arrive at the church early enough to get a pew where you can all sit together.

8. Before Mass: Make sure your children genuflect.

9. During Mass: Do not let them lean their bottoms on the pew seat. Warn them twice. Lightly spank your preschoolers with your Missal. That's why it's so big.

10. After Mass: Have a quick meeting with your spouse over coffee. How did it go? What went well? What didn't go well? What can we change for next week?

Meeting with spouse

What went well at Mass?

_____

_____

_____

What did not go well?

_____

_____

_____

Specific changes for next Sunday:

_____

_____

_____

_____

End of Pew   End of Pew

— — — — — — — — —

The second week

1. Tell your children that you would love to reward their good behavior with doughnuts or treats after Mass. But if they misbehave, they will not get a doughnut.

2. Practice two days this week, as you did last week.

3. Fine-tune your seating strategy with your spouse if needed.

4. If you are not praying as a family every day, start now. Make all the children kneel down. Start with two decades of the rosary, and then gradually add more until you pray five decades. The very little ones (under age four) won't be able to kneel through all five decades, but don't let them run around the room.

5. Saturday: Reflect upon last Sunday morning. How did it go? Now is the time to fix it. Find their shoes and lay out their church clothes tonight so tomorrow morning will go smoother.

6. Sunday morning: Be strong. You will still feed the kids breakfast, but once you get inside the church, make an example of someone. You are in control of your world.

You have zero tolerance for looking around, turning around, bottoms on pew seats while kneeling, or sitting while everyone else is standing. Give one warning and that's it. The second time someone misbehaves, pick up the little miscreant under the arms and physically carry him or her out the doors of the church. A spanking, by the father if possible, is most effective. Speak firmly after the spanking, but do not yell. Make the child genuflect when coming back to your pew.

7. Plan for discipline. Plan on leaving during Mass to spank a child. Expect it. God wants you to discipline your child, not sit there during the prayers and readings. Don't worry—God will give you thousands of other opportunities to sit through an entire Mass, if you build a foundation of good behavior now. This is the second week of your new behavior plan, and the kids will try to test your limits. They want to slouch back to their old behavior.

You have to be prepared to discipline your children. Your thoughts:

_____

_____

_____

8. Yes indeed, you are micromanaging them! They are little, and they are not used to behaving well. Monitor them closely at Mass, and it will get easier. You may have a strong desire to just sit through Mass. Is all this parental micromanaging being taken much too seriously? My answer: Invest in active parenting in the pew now, and you'll have more peaceful Masses for the rest of your life.

9. It's better for the father to do the spankings, as mentioned above. After Dad removes an errant child, Mom can direct

the remaining children toward the liturgical action at the altar. It works better if Dad is the "muscle." After the misbehaving child calms down, Dad should bring him or her back to the pew.

10. After Mass: who gets doughnuts? Who doesn't? If someone had borderline behavior, make them wait five minutes before eating their treat.

Meeting with spouse

What went well at Mass?

_____
_____
_____
_____

What did not go well?

_____
_____
_____
_____

Specific changes for next Sunday:

_____
_____
_____
_____

End of Pew

End of Pew

The third week

1. More of the same. Expect to leave during Mass to spank a child. Increase your vigilance. Use the rear-view mirror method: You look in your rear-view mirror about every three to five seconds while driving. At Holy Mass, do not go more than ten to twenty seconds without eyeing your kids. Sometimes you can turn your head just a little and watch for movement with your peripheral vision.

2. Watch for lazy feet. While standing or kneeling, young feet tend to slide up the kneeler or lean forward. Gently tap their legs. Tell them to sit/kneel up straight. Remember, about every ten or twenty seconds you should look at all your children. Put your hand on her head and turn it forward. Tap his leg and point to the kneeler. You are striving for dignity and respect—and *focused* attention on the Holy Sacrifice. Use gentle but firm hands to push their hands down or turn their heads.

3. Notice that much of this discipline—remember the root of the word has to do with order and correction—much of this discipline is non-verbal. This is necessary because of the reverent silence at Holy Mass, but it is also good for the children to see that authority is real; it exists whether Mom or Dad say anything or not. It is not simply a spoken thing.

Meeting with spouse

What went well at Mass?

_____

_____

_____

_____

What did not go well?

_____

_____

_____

_____

Specific changes for next Sunday:

_____

_____

_____

_____

End of Pew — — — — — — — — — — — End of Pew

The fourth week

1. Bump up the rewards and explain things more. If you've done everything in this book up to now, you should see at least some improvement from all but your youngest and highest-maintenance toddler. Explain different parts of the Mass to your school-aged children and make sure they each have their own Missal. Focus on a child's good behavior and point it out to the rest of the children after Mass, but never *compare* your children to each other—this does more harm than good.

2. You are not alone. Continue praying to your patron saint as you work on your children's behavior for Sunday Mass.

3. When infractions become rare, you may even begin to give them two warnings at that point instead of one. But if they slack off, revert back to one warning.

Take a minute to look back at your "Meeting with Spouse" from week 1. Compare your notes from that week to today. How have things improved from week 1 to week 4?
Your thoughts:

_____

_____

_____

4. A troublesome child: You probably have one child who simply will not respond much to your discipline. If you've already taken the child out of the same Mass twice for spankings, a third time will not be effective. Change your punishment. Remind your child, if he or she is old enough to receive Holy Communion, that our Lord wants to rest in the child's heart. Jesus wants the child to behave. (Don't forbid Holy Communion because of misbehavior—this could build up scrupulosity. However, the child should not go to the Communion rail angry.) After Mass, temporarily take away something they enjoy. Another good strategy is to make fidgety children kneel still for five to ten minutes after Mass. Be sure to tell them they are there because they did not kneel still during Mass.

    Meeting with spouse

What went well at Mass?

_____

_____

_____

_____

What did not go well?

_____

_____

_____

_____

Specific changes for next Sunday:

_____

_____

_____

_____

Final word

I saved the best for last. This astonishes me every time I see it happen.

Each of my children began behaving better at Mass about two weeks after they made their first Holy Communion. God in the Blessed Sacrament changes people. Your children will have the grace to act appropriately at Mass after receiving our Lord Himself. Saint John Bosco said that the best way to educate young people is to give them opportunities for frequent Confession and Holy Communion.[47]

Catholics are truly blessed. God Himself enters into our children and helps them behave.

It becomes obvious that this is through no work of ours; it is purely God working in them. Lean on our Eucharistic Lord and ask Him to help you discipline your children. Offer your children up to Him, and ask Him to give you the endurance you need to get through Sunday Mass. After all, it's His house, His sacrifice (and yours!), and it is really His Presence that you receive. God will help you, if you are serious about changing your children's behavior and you persevere.

Parenting not only involves raising children to be good people, but to be citizens of Heaven in the next life with God. Your children are a gift to you from God; He entrusted their souls to you. You are the one who needs to raise them and return them to Him. God expects you to teach your children how to love.

What does this really mean? It means there is no special "knack" to parenting. If you are a mother or a father, you already have the ability to raise your children well. Don't just encourage good behavior, expect it. God does not command the impossible. You can do this!

Drive around and look for the best schools if you wish. But if you really want to find the best teacher for your young children, look in the mirror.

Rely on God's mercy. Rely on the intercession of the Blessed Virgin Mary. When you are exasperated, pray to your children's guardian angels. They are on your side. You are not alone! Sunday Mass can be a truly rewarding experience—even if you have to spend a lot of it turning your four-year-old's head toward the front of the church, and tapping your eight-year-old's leg—because you are working to instill reverence in your children. Reverence toward the God who made them and who loves them. God loves you and He wants you to keep coming to Sunday Mass. He wants you to join your heart to His sacrifice. He wants you to train your children's hearts to love His Sacred Heart.

Get back to basics when life seems complicated. Who made you? God made you. Why? Because He loves you, and He wants you to serve Him in this life, and be happy with Him forever in the next.

Heaven! *That* is where your family really belongs. Do you want to save souls? Do you want to go to Heaven and be happy with God forever? Do you want to bring others with you? Start with your own children. Holy Mass is Christ's sacrifice applied for us today. In other words, it is a taste of Heaven. It is proof that God loves you.

In the middle of Pop Tarts, dirty clothes, and lost shoes on Sunday morning, getting to Heaven is what really matters.

---

[47] Johnston, *Voice,* p. 103

Selected Bibliography

Adler, Mortimer, *Great Ideas from the Great Books.* New York: Washington Square Press, 1963.

Allers, Rudolph, *Forming Character in Adolescents.* Fort Collins, CO: Roman Catholic Books, originally published 1940.

—. *Self Improvement.* Fort Collins, CO: Roman Catholic Books, orig. pub. 1938.

Bode, Carl, ed., *American Life in the 1840s.* New York: Anchor Books, 1967.

Catechism of the Catholic Church. Liguori, MO: Liguori Publications, 1994.

The Catechism of the Council of Trent. Rockford, IL: TAN Books and Publishers, Inc., 1982.

Chapin, John, ed., *The Book of Catholic Quotations.* Fort Collins, CO: Roman Catholic Books. Original publ. 1956, copyright renewed 1984 by Farrar, Straus & Giroux, Inc.

Dobson, James, *The Strong-Willed Child.* Wheaton, IL: Tyndale House Publishing, Inc., 1985.

Dogmatic Canons and Decrees. Rockford, IL: TAN Books and Publishers, Inc., 1977.

Flannery, Austin, ed., *Vatican Council II: The Conciliar and Post Conciliar Documents.* Northport, NY: Costello Publishing Company, 1987.

Hammond, Colleen, *Dressing With Dignity.* Rockford, IL: TAN Books and Publishers, Inc., 2005.

Hock, Rev. Conrad, *The Four Temperaments.* Milwaukee, WI: The Pallottine Fathers & Brothers, Inc., 1962, reprinted 2002.

Integrity: Raising Your Children. Kansas City, MO: Angelus Press, 1995.

The Heart of the Mass. Kansas City, MO: Sarto House, 1997

Johnston, Francis, *The Voice of the Saints.* Rockford, IL: TAN Books and Publishers, Inc., 1986.

Leman, Kevin, *The Birth Order Book.* New York: Dell Publishing, 1985.

Montessori, Maria, *The Mass Explained to Children.* Fort Collins, CO: Roman Catholic Books, orig. pub. 1932.

Pope Pius XII, *Mediator Dei*. November 20, 1947. From The Holy See's web site. http://www.vatican.va/holy_father/pius_xii/encyclicals/documents/hf_p-xii_enc_20111947_mediator-dei_en.html.

The Summa Theologica of St. Thomas Aquinas. Westminster, MD: Christian Classics, orig. copyright 1948.

von Hildebrand, Dietrich, *Liturgy and Personality*. Manchester, NH: Sophia Institute Press, 1990.

Wickens, Rev. Paul, *Handbook for Parents*. Long Prairie, MN: The Neumann Press, 1987.

Rafka
Press

Uplifting Families —
One Book at a Time

Visit us online for more Catholic literature.
www.rafkapress.com

www.ingramcontent.com/pod-product-compliance
Lightning Source LLC
LaVergne TN
LVHW091226080426
835509LV00009B/1192

* 9 7 8 0 9 7 7 9 6 2 8 4 6 *